VOLUME III

Improving Classroom Practice Through a Culturally-Centered Education Program

A Guide for All Teachers

by

Maxine Newsome, Ph.D.

MODEL ALTERNATIVE SCHOOL SERVICES PROFESSIONAL DEVELOPMENT SERIES FOR EXCELLENCE IN TEACHING AND LEARNING

This series is dedicated to my late husband and friend, Thomas Newsome I, who was the wind beneath my wings in living through the topics and events of this series.

Copyright © 2012 by Maxine Newsome.
All rights reserved, including the right of reproduction in whole or in part or in any form.
ISBN   978-0-9839496-2-6
Published by MASS

Please visit www.schoolin.org for further consultation and inquiry.

MASS
Professional Development Series for Excellence in Teaching and Learning

CONTENTS

Volume I

The Context of Classroom Practice in American Schools

Volume II

Improving Classroom Practice Through Culturally-Inclusive Classroom Management

Volume III

Improving Classroom Practice Through a Culturally-Centered Education Program

Volume IV

Improving Classroom Practice Through Culturally-Transformative Teaching

"As the editor of this book and as a licensed educator in the public school system, I have deepened my understanding of what my population of students will require for growing through their transitions in my classrooms with joy and a sense of recognition—and of how I can be the greater teacher that I have not yet had the courage to be.

We all have to learn to come from the places that others come from and to be guests in those places, and to teach to those places in ourselves while holding them open for the interactions of others. With the authority of a caring friend on the journey to genuine and masterful teaching, the work will bring your thinking as an educator in today's world to another, more encompassing platform—so that we can all enjoy these new places of beauty together."

Erjan Slavin, Teacher, Author, Poet, Editor
--Peekskill, NY

"Building cross-cultural understanding for a caring world through excellence in classroom practice..."

Overview of the MASS Professional Development Series

"We can change the world!" is clearly a belief of many young people and is a major reason why many decide to enter the field of education. At no point in time has the challenge set forth in this rallying cry been more relevant than today as we look toward a Twenty-First Century world.

Now, the work begins. It involves the way that you, the teachers of America, take on this challenge through the practices that you employ in your classrooms. It has to do with your insight and ability to help students from multiple cultural backgrounds to learn, interact with each other, understand each other, and to care for and about each other.

Changing the world may seem like a lofty goal…but when you think about it, given the number of students with whom you will interact over the course of your career, you are positioned to change the lives of many. You will have students as your captive audience for more hours than any other of society's institutions, including the family. The way that you use your influence with your students in the classroom can make a lasting difference in what and how well they will learn, in their perceptions and attitudes, and in the way they will go out into the world and relate to others in the larger society. In this sense, as a classroom teacher, you can create a culturally-inclusive classroom to serve as a microcosm for building respect, understanding, and caring in a multicultural world. The power to change the society resides with you, a dedicated teacher, who nurtures your students to be the influential leaders of tomorrow. The lofty goal of changing the world will come only when you have the vision of what it can be, and acknowledge the powerful role and opportunity that you have through your teaching to improve societal conditions.

The Cultural Dimensions of Classroom Practice

The Model Alternative School Services' *Professional Development Series for Excellence in Teaching and Learning* emphasizes culturally-compatible classroom practice as the foundation for excellence in teaching and learning. The belief expressed throughout the series is that culture is integral to the actual practices in American classrooms. The approach is to make the theory and research on effective teaching, classroom management, and multicultural education more accessible and usable by connecting it in practical ways to daily classroom practice.

The four-volume series aims to have you become what Henry Giroux refers to as a transforming intellectual. A major step in the transformation is to have you begin to learn about dominant mainstream culture—something that has been omitted in multicultural discourse. The series seeks to develop your cultural and pedagogical knowledge and competence so that you can display your developing expertise in the classroom to assure learning excellence for all of your students.

The series proposes that students be taught the dominant American mainstream culture, its manifestations and ramifications, with full understanding of why they are learning it, and how they can transform and make use of this knowledge in their lives to make a difference. In other words, students learn the dominant "culture of power" thoroughly and in depth as a means to an end, so that they have essential knowledge and insight into the dominant culture, and the willingness and readiness to change "what is" toward a more embracing international culture.

The educational content, level of critical inquiry about schooling, and classroom practice strategies developed in these four volumes are not being taught in today's K-12 classrooms nor are they being taught at the university level in the schools of education. As a result of the changing face and direction of America and the void in teacher education, this professional development series is relevant, and in fact, crucial. The series is concerned with improving classroom practice on the part of beginning as well as veteran teachers. Each volume in the series is both conceptual and practical in offering original and fresh insights that are applicable in today's classroom settings.

Your Journey Through the Series

The complete MASS *Professional Development Series* gives you the basics in knowledge and skill to operate a culturally-inclusive classroom. Volume I sets the stage for improving classroom practice by providing information to develop your cultural competence and understanding of the cultural context of American classroom practice; Volume II outlines the necessary ingredients for structuring and managing a culturally-inclusive classroom; Volume III helps you design and implement a culturally-centered education program, and Volume IV presents a comprehensive model of culturally-transformative teaching for you to assure excellence in student learning.

After you complete the three modules in Volume I of the series, you should have a basic foundation and the requisite cultural competence for effective classroom practice. *Module One* offers some insights into why classroom practice that has an aim of building cultural understanding is needed. You learn, in *Module Two*, how American schools and classrooms came to be as they are as you hear the stories of the representative cultural groups who are the focus of the series: Native American, Latino American, Asian American, African American and Arab-Muslim American. Related to *Modules One* and *Two* is the perspective that you gain in *Module Three*, which enables you to examine schools and classrooms through a lens that you might not have considered before. This third module, which introduces you to critical pedagogy, calls for you to consider the contextual and historical information from *Modules One* and *Two* and your emerging knowledge of what goes on in classrooms in relationship to what you would like your own classroom to be. *Module Three* concludes Volume I, the cultural context of classroom practice.

The background you will gain in Volume I will be essential in your effort to improve classroom practice; therefore, if you choose to read only one of the books, this one should be your choice. If you choose other books or the complete series, the cultural context for the series as presented in Volume I is highly recommended for your initial study. After studying the three modules in this volume, you will surely be motivated to alter what you have been doing and apply what you have learned to more effectively embrace all of your students. For specific ways to improve classroom practice, you will benefit from studying the complete four-volume series. The three practical volumes will explain how to go about teaching to embrace all of your students. And, if you choose, you will have an opportunity to practice and further develop your cultural and pedagogical expertise through the professional development materials and personalized sessions with MASS consultants.

Volume II of the series gives you a thorough presentation of ways to employ culturally-inclusive practices as you manage the classroom. The four modules in Volume II take you from start to finish in designing and managing your classroom in culturally-compatible ways. In *Module One*, you learn how to set forth the core principles to formulate the attitudes and behaviors, which you and your students aim to work toward in your daily classroom interactions. It is these goals or standards for behavior that give direction to the management of your classroom. *Module Two* is considered to be the essential classroom management module of this volume. It helps you set up your classroom, induct your students into the classroom environment, and teach the procedures necessary to enable students to work together. Once the classroom is set up, you have the structure for orchestrating your classroom with style, sensitivity and caring. The material outlined in *Module Three* provides approaches for you to consider as you seek to build a caring classroom community. In spite of the foundation that you establish, and the way that you structure and orchestrate your classroom, however, there will be some instances in which you will need to assist students who, from time to time, may have difficulty meeting expectations and staying on course with he established core principles of the classroom community. You learn various ways to prevent and address student misbehavior in *Module Four*.

The educational program can be viewed as the substance of teaching and learning. Volume III of the series retains this viewpoint; however, it goes on further in using the educational program as a vehicle to promote cross-cultural understanding among diverse students and families. *Module One* helps you design and implement a culturally-centered education program and *Module Two* helps you connect the educational program to your work with families. A variety of methods for communicating with families and a comprehensive approach to involving families in their child's learning will be emphasized in *Module Two*.

Moving into the delivery of the curriculum, you have the opportunity in Volume IV to embrace multiple cultures through culturally-transformative teaching, a comprehensive systematic approach to precise teaching. Culturally-transformative teaching develops and refines your teaching skill, builds cross-cultural understanding, and assures excellence in student learning. The lesson framework and the teaching principles, as they are outlined in this volume, can form the basis for a complete school or district-wide teacher development and evaluation system. Your effective use of the framework and principles transforms dominant culture material and elevates your thinking and the thinking of your students.

Building cross-cultural understanding through effective classroom practice calls for you to dismantle old ways of doing things in your classroom, and to replace them with culturally compatible practices. Your ability to assure excellence in learning for all students depends on your cultural competence and commitment to operate from a foundation of cultural inclusiveness. Since American classrooms are held to a dominant culture model, you are sure to find yourself engaged in continuous examination of your belief system about classrooms, schools, and about society itself. Your professional and personal growth rests on your openness to questioning, challenging, and ultimately of changing what is to a more open and embracing educational program and environment. These professional development materials, in combination with the accompanying lectures, seminars, and personalized consultant services are dedicated to helping you become a thoughtful discerning teacher who is dedicated to improving classroom practice.

In many ways, I think of the material you are about to read as a memoir of my life as an educator. After an extended career in teaching and administration in urban, suburban, and rural schools and school districts, I have participated directly in teaching and guiding others through the experiences described in the four-volume series. These experiences have taken place in both mainstream and culturally-diverse settings and have also included consultant services in various geographical regions of the U.S. I have numerous stories to tell about my classroom experiences over a broad educational career—and this professional development series presents an opportunity to tell many of them. Some stories are more personal involving my son, who is an integral part of MASS—Model Alternative School Services—my precious and precocious nieces and other relatives that I have been honored to teach and watch blossom into caring competent adults. Others are stories about friends and colleagues whom I have been fortunate to learn from along the way, and students whom I have taught from elementary school to graduate school. My recollection of each experience has added to my understanding of schooling and of classroom practice.

Also, the research and authorities cited in the series are those whose writings I have known, loved, and lived with over time. Over the years, these "best practices" have served me well in my work in numerous classrooms from the kindergarten to university level and in professional development settings. Educators like me have respected and incorporated the concepts and principles of such noted authorities as Jerome Bruner, Jacob Kounin, Henry Giroux, John Goodlad, Grant Wiggins, Howard Gardner, and Madelyn Hunter in our classroom practices even in the face of more recent theories. These icons in the field of education didn't just give us new trends or speculative ideas—they gave us sound concepts and principles for practices that actually work in classrooms. These authors are referred to here as masters and their writings as classics because they still set the standard for the field. It was because of these and other influential educators that I was able get better and better at my craft and consequently to influence the learning and lives of my students. The topics that I have written about are referred to in this series as evidence-based, because they present clear evidence of how the concepts and principles expressed in the writing of these and other authorities actually work in practice.

I have learned from the experts, but I have also learned from active practical research in my own classroom and in numerous other classrooms from teachers with whom I have been fortunate to work and to learn from along the way. I want us to take this journey through the series together—and I want you to conclude that the series' approaches to classroom practice have been formulated in an accordance with sound evidence-based theory, research, and practices that have stood the test of time. Hopefully, you can benefit from my experience and avoid many of the trials and errors that overwhelmed me in my early days of teaching. Think of me as your mentor as I walk along side and speak to you telling my story as we go.

VOLUME III

CONTENTS

Introduction to Volume III…2

Module One

Designing a Culturally-Centered Education Program…5

Module Two

Engaging Families as Partners in the Culturally-Centered Education Program…40

The MASS Professional Development Series in Review…72

Introduction to Volume III

Improving Classroom Practice Through a Culturally-Centered Education Program

This volume highlights the ways in which knowledge to build cross-cultural understanding is vital and enhancing to classroom practice. The broad factors which distinguish the world's cultures and the distinctions among cultural groups were discussed in earlier volumes. In this volume you continue to build your cultural competence as you add your developing knowledge of these world cultures to your educational program. The focus is on shaping the curriculum experienced in American schools to embrace multiple cultures and points of view.

To begin it helps to build a bridge from where K-12 curriculum in American schools has been in terms of cross-cultural emphasis and excellence in learning to where it is today and the twists and turns that it has taken over the past half century. When I started teaching, the curriculum (course of study and textbooks) was less prescribed than today. Teachers had more discretion in planning creatively what to teach as long as it was within the Anglo-American culture paradigm. During that time, there was no such thing as multicultural content or even multicultural illustrations in textbooks. The stories, selections of content and manner in which they were conveyed, the characters and the way they were portrayed, were all examples of what this society wanted its school children to know and be like.

Gradually, various curricula and instructional materials began to include multicultural pictures and concepts but the message continued to be Anglo-American. Even a modest attempt toward multiculturalism prompted a backlash from those whose goal was to maintain an Anglo-American dominant-culture society. Among the more recent leaders of this attempt was E.D. Hirsch who in his book, Cultural Literacy (Hirsch, 1987), argued that teaching mainstream culture was essential, particularly for "culturally-deprived" students who needed access to information that middle class students receive in their daily encounters with other literate persons. This book was given so much attention that Hirsch published a dictionary and series of books for elementary children which set forth a cultural literacy curriculum for kindergarten through grade six titled, What Your Kindergartener Should Know, What Your First Grader Should Know, etc. Cultural literacy as outlined by Hirsch was not so much concerned with improving educational quality and student learning but with assuring the preservation of Anglo-American culture and traditions which he saw slipping away without a set of core knowledge concepts that all school children know and embrace.

In the late 1980's, even though I agreed with Hirsch's call for a general curriculum and standards to give direction to the learning process, the premise upon which Hirsch based his plea for cultural literacy was more constrained than I had envisioned. In my earlier book, Privileged Class (1992), I reiterated the need for substantive content to replace the skills-based "laissez faire anything goes" approach that seemed to predominate in schools at the time. I saw a need for a clearly defined curriculum and standards of excellence for all students. However, as I discussed extensively in Volume I of this series, facility with and a thorough understanding of dominant-culture information would serve as a means to an end. I am calling for this attitude throughout the series, for teachers and students to understand and analyze dominant-culture material from multiple perspectives, and then modify and broaden the material to include the perspectives of those whose voices have been excluded.

In this era of accountability, we are faced with curricula and materials geared to helping students pass high stakes competency tests. This state-wide emphasis in many locales influences classroom practice to such an extent that the school day is centered on testing. Instead of teaching, teachers are faced with the priority of preparing students to pass state-mandated dominant-culture competency tests. Such inflexibility has made it difficult enough to teach what is deemed necessary to pass the tests, not to mention thinking about ways to include other cultural orientations and perspectives.

This volume of the series describes ways that you can overcome the curriculum limitations that have been imposed on teachers over these years. It continues the goal of building students' cross-cultural understanding as it helps you create a culturally-centered education program. *Module One* concentrates on the substance of the program by offering ways to broaden and shape the curriculum and assessment process in the interest of cultural inclusion, and *Module Two* concentrates on implementing the curriculum through home-school communication and family involvement.

With assessment as the focal point of the educational program, the first module calls for authentic culturally-enriched performance-based learning and assessment tasks. These tasks are to assure student competency with dominant-culture material in a broader more culturally enhanced arrangement. *Module Two* helps you put it all together by structuring families' meaningful participation in their child's education program. It shows you how to employ frequent ongoing communication with families and how to interact meaningfully and sensitively with them both to enhance student motivation and to promote cross-cultural understanding through their meaningful involvement in the culturally-centered education program.

On my many occasions, while working in schools and as a parent myself, I have learned that every family is concerned about two things related to classroom practice: the well-being of their children and the quality of education the children are receiving. As teachers, then, we are on solid ground when we also keep these two essentials uppermost in our minds in our communication and interactions with students and families. The relationships that we can build with families and the insights about their children's lives that we can gain will aid us as we pursue educational excellence and build our students' level of cross-cultural knowledge and understanding.

Module One

Designing a Culturally-Centered Education Program

Opening Scenario…6

Key Concepts…9

<u>Topics Covered in This Module:</u>

- How the Education Program Can Support Classroom Practice to Build Cross-Cultural Understanding…9

- Multiple Approaches to Student Learning: Principles and Concepts…11

    Differing Styles and Perspectives on Thinking and Learning…12

    Accommodating Diversity in Learning…13

- Student Performance as the Centerpiece of Learning …15

    Authentic Assessment: The Three P's…17

    Other Methods of Measuring Student Performance…19

- A Curriculum to Develop World-Wide Perspectives and Cross-Cultural Understanding…20

    Expanding Curriculum for World-Wide Perspectives…20

    The Curriculum Approach…22

    Subject Matter Recommendations to Promote Cross-Cultural Understanding…22

    The Teacher Read Aloud: An Essential Resource for Building Cross-Cultural Understanding…26

- Structuring the Education Program…32

    Long Range Planning…32

    Mid-Range or Unit Planning…33

    Short Range Planning…34

Classroom Teachers Talk It Over…35

Summary of Module One…36

Opening Scenario (Afterthoughts)…37

Questions/Activities…37

Looking in Classrooms…38

Recommendations for Further Reading…39

Opening Scenario

Students in a secondary U.S. history classroom are studying the Lincoln-Douglas Debates and the most predominant issue in the presidential election of 1858. The issue and debate were about slavery and whether it should continue to exist in United States. The students, many whom are African Americans, have the opportunity to listen to a dramatic reconstruction of these debates to hear the actual words of Abraham Lincoln in his "House Divided" speech and the rebuttal or counter argument of Steven A. Douglas, in which he presents his argument for the widely held view at the time of retaining slavery and such notions of "slaves as property," "states' rights," and the "rights of the people" which at that time included white people only.

The students found out that these debates, referred to as the debates that defined America, set the stage for other presidential debates to follow. Consequently, as part of their study, students were also given the opportunity to compare the Lincoln-Douglas presidential debates to subsequent presidential debates, and specifically to the arguments set forth in the 2008 presidential debates—the partisanship, the truth-twisting, the name calling, etc. It didn't take long for heightened interest to take hold in the class.

Under the teacher's guidance, students began to study, analyze and make comparisons between the two eras. This comparison of 1858 politics with 2008 politics, a 150 year expanse of time, made sense to them. They were excited, interested, and even angry, mainly because they had never before been given the opportunity to learn in depth about information that had relevance to their lives and to study it from multiple perspectives. They could see that the Lincoln-Douglas debates had remarkable resemblance to today's campaign speeches. After learning that the roles of the democratic and republican parties have been reversed in this century, with many democrats becoming republicans and vice versa, they decided to listen more carefully to the 2008 speeches and debates, and commentary between the republican and democratic positions in the campaign for the presidency. The comments from students were overwhelmingly positive as many simply commented, "What a way to study history!"

How would you describe the excitement of these students and what do you think prompted the excitement?
What curriculum-based strategies did the teacher employ? What information was needed and is this generally taught in high school classes?
What perceptions do you have about a culturally-centered education program as you begin this module?
As you prepare to become or continue your role as a teacher in today's world of culturally diverse classrooms, you may wonder how the education program can help you conduct your classroom in culturally competent ways.

This module begins Volume III of the Professional Development Series, which identifies the attributes of a culturally-centered education program as the substance of classroom practice. It shows how the education program influences what takes place in classrooms, and it makes it clear that what and how students are taught can have substantial impact on their enthusiasm, day-to-day classroom interactions, and their excellence in learning. The two modules in Volume III, the education program in *Module One* and the involvement of families in *Module Two*, need to be considered together. The topics and modules flow together and support each other. This first module calls for shaping the district's curriculum to give priority to world knowledge and to building cross-cultural understanding. Authentic performance assessment presented first in this module and extended in *Module Two* is the centerpiece of the education program. With assessment as the focal point, what students learn throughout the year is targeted toward the end of year assessments. At this celebration of learning students, with their families in attendance, demonstrate and are assessed in visible ways on what they have learned during the year. Families, as you will see in this volume, are meaningfully involved in their child's education program as true partners in helping their children prepare for the assessments.

As you study this module, you should focus on answering the following key questions:

- How can the education program support classroom practice to build cross-cultural understanding?

- What are the multiple ways that students learn, and what are some approaches that you can use to promote learning and cross-cultural understanding?

- What are student exhibitions of learning and how you can make student performance the highlight of your educational program?

- What are some ways to adapt the curriculum to foster multiple cultural perspectives?

- How can you make the reading aloud of multicultural books the focal point of your daily academic routine to build cross-cultural understanding?

- How do you target and structure the education program to enable students to demonstrate their learning and level of cross-cultural understanding during end-of-year performance exhibitions?

Key Concepts

cognitive style ~ field dependent/independent ~ impulsive/reflective thinking ~ status differences ~ high status principle ~ visibility/invisibility ~ accountability ~ whole-part-whole principle ~ multiple intelligences theory ~ metacognition ~ sensory channels ~ emancipatory knowledge ~ right/left brain hemispheres ~ performance exhibition ~ authentic assessment ~ formative/summative assessment ~ dialog assessment ~ rubric ~ high stakes testing ~ reliability ~ validity ~ norm/criterion referenced test ~ Piaget's stages ~ expanding horizon's curriculum ~ Eurocentric curriculum ~ multiple intelligences ~ declarative/procedural/conditional knowledge ~ long/mid/short range planning ~ 3P's (portfolio/project/performance) ~ cultural bias ~ structure of a discipline ~ curriculum guide

How a Culturally-Centered Education Program Can Support Classroom Practice to Build Cross-Cultural Understanding

The education program is inextricably intertwined with classroom practice. A culturally-centered education program with a world-wide focus, then, broadens and enhances the quality of classroom practice. In this professional development series the education program serves as the source for obtaining cross-cultural knowledge and as the resource for creating a culturally-attuned classroom community. The emphasis is on shaping the formal mandated dominant-culture curriculum to embrace other cultures, an effort that is sure to be enlightening for you and your students.

There are two different cultural frames of reference that can guide you in shaping the curriculum beyond the dominant culture standard. It is useful to note, for example, that western cultures such as the United States are typically geared to out-of-context learning arrangements in which the students learn certain concepts in a classroom setting for the purpose of applying their learning later in real-world settings. Non-western less industrialized cultures, on the other hand, tend toward in-context learning arrangements where both instruction and application take place together in real-life settings under the guidance of a teacher. Curriculum theorists have pondered these two different frames of reference over time. Clearly, out-of-context arrangements predominate in American culture but by shaping the curriculum you can employ in-context opportunities for students to learn and apply their knowledge in a real-world context as well.

Other frames of reference can also help you create a culturally-centered education program. These frames of reference contrast the Eurocentric dominant-culture perspective with alternative perspectives which comes to us from the five representative cultural groups that we track throughout the series. Your study of these groups beginning in Volume I, can point you to some little known, often overlooked, stories about Native Americans, African Americans, Latin American, Asian Americans, and Arab Americans that you can bring forth and build into your educational program. As one example, to provide the accurate story of Native Americans, you would contrast information that depicts the diversity and accomplishments of the Indian Nations *prior to the coming of Europeans,* with the stereotypical savage of the plains or feathers and tepees misrepresentation still found in many textbooks and classroom practices. Today most teachers and students know about Martin Luther King, Jr., as the black American hero but few know about his life, hardships, and achievements in depth. Fewer still know about other African Americans in other fields, black musicians remarkable creative ability in jazz music, for example. So, another modification to the curriculum that you can make would be to tell the African American story in a non-superficial way. Similarly, few people know that Latin Americans were the first to settle in the vast western territory which, after war and conquest, was annexed to the United States. The story about how this territory ultimately became the states of Texas, New Mexico, Colorado, Arizona, California, among others needs to be known and shared in the interest of truth and respect to the heritage of Latin Americans. As another example, it is generally believed that most Asian American families value education and are highly motivated so much so that their zeal for learning and achievement should be acknowledged and valued for its contribution to the American experience. For a final example from the five representative cultural groups, Middle Eastern families are the group most under suspicion and surveillance at the dawn of the 21st Century because the World Trade Center tragedy on September 11, 2001. However, through a multiple perspective approach it can be instructive to draw parallels to show how and why other cultural groups also faced and overcame similar discrimination at different points in American history. These often neglected truths about Native Americans, African Americans, Latin Americans, Asian Americans, and

Americans from Middle Eastern countries can be at the center of your educational program to broaden students' knowledge base.

The perspective that you can provide on these cultural groups by shaping the curriculum in the interest of portraying a true picture of their lives and accomplishments will add to students' store of cross-cultural knowledge. Still, the most essential thing that you can do to honor other cultures is to take every opportunity to continuously teach students that the course of study in American classrooms is essentially Eurocentric, centered on Anglo-European culture, and that there are other equally important domains of learning. The exclusive presence of the Eurocentric dominant-culture curriculum can cause students and teachers alike to view this form of knowledge as the only legitimate point of view and to consider all other knowledge as an add-on of lesser quality and value. From such thinking, prejudice can easily form in the mind of the student. When students are freed from seeing the dominant-culture paradigm as "the only way," their eyes are open to interpreting the world in multiple ways and to appreciating the diversity of students in their classrooms and of peoples throughout the world, their knowledge bases and their ways of doing and being.

Students need a culturally-centered curriculum where knowledge embraces multiple cultural orientations and is open to multiple viewpoints. But this can only happen through your own cultural competence. Cultural competence as it relates to the education program requires you to be knowledgeable and open to learning beyond what has been common knowledge in American schools. The culturally-centered education program delineated in this section calls for you to know in depth what you are supposed to teach so that you can be guided by essential truths in the form of general principles rather be bound by isolated detailed bits of information as it often appears in textbooks. You need to be able to examine the mandated curriculum for its truth in depicting other cultures and ways of viewing the world. Then, you need to be able to help your students scrutinize and question what they are learning. When you and your students are diligent in analyzing the portrayal of other cultures in the education program, you can then make appropriate adjustments and enhancements to clarify and broaden students' cultural knowledge and understanding.

Multiple Approaches to Student Learning:
Principles and Concepts

Knowing how different students learn and process information is essential to planning and implementing a culturally-centered education program. Without such knowledge, you are likely to center the learning of all students on the dominant mainstream culture paradigm and the way that you were taught. This module looks at some dimensions of student learning that are relevant for teaching multicultural populations, cognitive style and status differences, in particular. It also offers methods associated with these dimensions that you can use to develop student thinking and learning: multiple intelligences, metacognitive considerations, and attending to different strategies that students use to process information.

Differing Styles and Perspectives on Thinking and Learning

The different ways in which people process information has come to be known in the educational literature as *cognitive style*. Cognitive style is independent from intelligence and, because there is evidence to suggest that cognitive style is influenced by one's culture, an understanding of its properties is important in a culturally-centered education program. This module looks at two continuums of cognitive style: field-dependent versus field-independent and reflective versus impulsive tendencies. **Field dependent** students tend to benefit from learning situations that are more holistic and imbedded in context, whereas ***field independent*** students tend toward learning situations that are independent of context and are presented in a linear step-by-step fashion. In general, European American students tend to be more field independent and Latin American, Native American, and African American students tend to be more field dependent (Baloche 1998, 41). Similarly, while some students tend to excel in tasks that require immediate analysis and learning situations based more on ***impulsive thinking,*** others tend to excel in tasks that require more ***reflective thinking,*** and the opportunity to develop alternatives before responding, areas which also have cultural implications.

The perceived status that a student has in a group of his or her peers can have considerable bearing on the student's classroom interactions and teachers may unwittingly promote ***status differences*** without this knowledge. In classroom interactions generally, students perceived to have high status are given more opportunities to participate and learn than students perceived to have low status. Consider, for example, an often used and seemingly innocuous classroom game called "Around the World." In this game the students, who already know the answers, are the beneficiaries of practice and status since it is these students who stay in the game and are applauded by the group. In contrast, the students who really need more practice and applause from their peers are eliminated from the game early on. In instances such as these where the objective is to win not learn, those who need more receive less. Also consider the ***high status principle*** which can operate this way in the group dynamic of classrooms. Students tend to see those who talk or contribute early in a group as more influential and to have higher status. Group members also tend to accord higher status and view the person who has talked the most, to have made the most important contributions, and the person who has talked the least, is accorded lower status and viewed as having made the least important contributions (Cohen, 1994, p.27). Also related to status in classroom practice is the notion of ***visibility and invisibility*** in culturally diverse classrooms. Some students may be visible initially because of the color of their skin, their dress, or their language, but if they are not valued and influential in the group, they can quickly take on a persona of invisibility.

Accommodating Diversity in Learning

Differences in these styles and perspectives have cultural competence implications. Teachers generally teach in a linear fashion devoid of context, and are socialized to think that the student who comes up with the answer the fastest is more intellectually competent than the student who benefits from context and takes more time. Cognitive style distinctions have contributed substantially to the understanding and approach that teachers can take to address cultural diversity in the classroom. In the past, IQ governed classroom practice and beliefs about students, but now greater recognition is being given to the style a student uses to process information and to other factors such as status differences within the group, and the multiple intelligences that students in all cultural groups possess to a greater or lesser degree.

Cultural competence asks you to teach in ways that encompass the cognitive styles of non-dominant as well as dominant culture students. To do this, it is important that you teach so as to include both the ***right and left-brain hemispheres.*** In dominant culture classrooms where teaching to the left hemisphere of the brain predominates, you understand that when you involve the right side, you are able to embrace the cognitive styles of other cultures as well. You also understand that similar to the field dependent-field independent paradigm, the right hemisphere grasps the whole picture more quickly and the left hemisphere is more amenable to details, and a linear step-by-step approach. The right and left brain styles and field dependent/field independent styles are encompassed in this series in its ***whole-part-whole principle*** which calls for having learners attend to the larger segment of learning in its holistic form before considering its parts. This principle and method of pedagogy are demonstrated thoroughly in Volume IV.

Your cultural competence would also be recognized by your ability to elevate students' status and visibility in the group. For example, if you give a low status student the opportunity to talk early and contribute with confidence in a group session, the student's status in the group may be elevated and the student perceived as more influential by his or her peers. Your role would be to find an area where a perceived low status student can excel, prepare the student to contribute successfully, and therefore become more influential in the group. (Baloche 1998, 51-52) You can also recognize the qualities that make students visible, and help the class recognize and value these students for who they are. At the same time, you can make an effort to discover why any student is reluctant to interact and contribute in class, and use finesse to get these hesitant students to participate at a pace that is comfortable for them. (McEwan, 2000, p. 157)

Howard Gardner (1983) in his groundbreaking work, *Frames of Mind: The Theory of Multiple Intelligences*, has contributed substantially to the current thinking in education about talent and ability that can be useful in addressing student diversity in learning. Through his theory of **multiple intelligences,** Gardner identified eight intelligences: linguistic, logical mathematical, musical, spatial, bodily-kinesthetic, interpersonal, intrapersonal, and naturalist intelligence and he is considering others. Gardner developed his theory by studying the variety of skills that are valued in society. For example, he noted that many people may not excel in verbal or analytical tasks, but do excel in getting along with others. This interpersonal skill of relating to others has served them well and, in some instances, has enabled them to be even more successful than their well-schooled counterparts. Other people have displayed an intrapersonal awareness of their own strengths and weaknesses and have capitalized on their strengths while minimizing their weaknesses. Gardner's theory has tremendous implications for us to understand and use to respond to the multiple approaches to learning among culturally diverse populations. His work takes us beyond simply valuing a student's ability to perform tasks that American schools' value such as reading, language, and mathematics to other intellectual tasks, valued equally if not more, by the broader society.

Much has been learned about productive ways in which you can develop students' intellectual ability, readiness for learning and the processes they use to learn how to learn. Your ability to develop students' thinking and learning skills is needed for all student populations and is a major indicator of both your pedagogical and cultural competence. For example, you should be able to develop students' intellectual capacities by bringing the students' mental faculties to the surface and then giving them multiple perspectives or models of thinking to aim for in mastering the material. Students' thought processes become conscious when you have them "think out loud" about their own thinking, a process referred to as **metacognition**. You should also be able to apply the elements of learning theory to help students accelerate their learning and retain what they learn. If you are a culturally-attuned teacher, for example, you plan lessons to accommodate the three **sensory channels** (visual, auditory, and kinesthetic) knowing that student learning in all cultural groups is strengthened when teaching captures all channels.

In essence then, as both a culturally and pedagogically competent teacher, you use visuals and multidimensional approaches to accommodate students' learning styles, you develop student's thought processes in all subjects by posing questions to them at the onset of learning, intermittently as learning proceeds, and at the end of a learning cycle, and you encourage your students to continuously question material for its truth, relevance, and applicability to multiple cultural orientations. You give students direct instruction in the processes of learning to develop their intellectual abilities so that they become habitually self-regulating and capable of monitoring their own progress and understanding, whether it is in reading a passage, writing a composition, or solving a problem. For example, you encourage students to stop during their study and ask themselves, "What is the meaning or relevance of the material for me in terms of my background and aspirations? How does the material relate to others with backgrounds unlike mine?" Then throughout the learning process you encourage students to continuously ask themselves, "Do I understand?" "Am I on the right track?" Am I extending my thinking beyond what has become common knowledge?" and obtain information or help and make adjustments as necessary. The attitude that you want to convey is that students must learn to monitor their own learning, to be confident and believe in their competence, to persevere in the face of challenges, and to view mistakes as obstacles to be overcome.

Insights into the nature of students' individual and cultural learning preferences increase our understanding of the learning process overall. When we clearly understand the nature and impact of such dimensions of learning as cognitive style and status relationships on diversity in learning, our approach to teaching is greatly enhanced and the nature of how we all learn takes on new significance. These preferences make it clear that no one size fits all. Now, when students come to us with cultural backgrounds other than the typical dominant-culture model we are no longer at a loss for what to do. The opportunity to work with a broad range of students becomes a welcomed challenge that we can handle successfully. Certainly, having alternative ways to look at students and their capabilities cannot help but expand the way that we engage and interact with them. Conscious consideration and development of student potential, their styles and preferences, and the intellectual processes associated with them help us teach all students how to learn.

Throughout this series the call is for you to be capable and alert to teaching directly what is needed at a given point in the classroom. Now that you have the background and know what is possible, I hope you see the rationale for being assertive, pedagogically and culturally competent, and not stand by and miss opportunities to intervene to assure that all of your students are successful. Hopefully, you also see the need to be vigilant and not acquiesce to textbook coverage or to teaching only the narrow range of content deemed appropriate in the mandated curriculum. Instead, I hope you will be committed to centering your education program on a broader more enhanced knowledge base which conveys multiple and alternative ways to view and learn about the world.

Student Performance as the Centerpiece of Learning

In this series authentic performance assessment serves as the centerpiece in the curriculum-teaching-assessment triad because of its overriding influence on all aspects of the education program. What students are expected to learn, the teaching to get them there, and the involvement of families to assist and support the program of learning are all centered on assessment, the performance exhibition at the end of the year. With the ***performance exhibition*** as the target, teachers begin with the end in mind—what students are expected to know and be able to demonstrate at the end of a cycle of learning or grade level.

When you know what you want students to be able to do at the end of a cycle of learning and communicate that expectation to students and their families, the learning goals are established and known, and all concerned can work together to assist students in achieving them. Performance exhibitions center and focus the curriculum and teaching by requiring students to be assessed on their competence in performing actual holistic tasks at the end of the school year. They enable you and your students to work productively toward authentic performances and to base day-to-day teaching and learning on students' growing understanding of the content and their ability to demonstrate the requisite knowledge and skills in their performances at year's end.

The backdrop for authentic performance assessment as delineated in this series is the early work of Grant Wiggins (Wiggins, 1989) who based his theory on such real-world performances as that of the athlete in "The Big Game" or the musician in "The Recital." Wiggins and his colleagues began the authentic assessment movement by challenging traditional assessment which they saw as simplistic and limiting in terms of measuring what students really need to be good at knowing and doing. Authentic measures not only monitor standards, but also set standards. Wiggins believes that you should "teach to the test." because, in authentic performance assessment, the test is a genuine representation of authentic learning and you are involved in designing the performances to be exhibited.

Since authentic assessment is concerned with assessing the quality of a student's products, procedures, or performances, they are more realistic than traditional tests. ***Authentic assessment*** in this context is concerned with having students perform exemplary tasks as evidence of what they know and can do. As Wiggins suggests, the authentic tasks and standards of performance that typically face writers, artists, scientists, community leaders, and historians are applied to the education program outlined in this series. The performances include such tasks as making presentations, writing essays and reports, reading and explaining literary works, performing experiments, and conducting research. These authentic processes and products are to be demonstrated and assessed in portfolios, projects, and "on-your feet" performances. Authentic assessments are based on pre-established criteria. To make authentic assessment fair and useful, distinctions in the quality of student performance is determined from clearly defined criteria spelled out on a ***rubric*** or checklist. These criteria are known in advance to students, their families, and the community at large. Student performance is evaluated and scored based on the scale and descriptors of the rubric. Over time, examples of actual student performances, in the form of videos, completed projects, and written documents can be compiled to express the rubric's qualities in visual concrete form through written documents, complete projects, and videos of performances.

Authentic assessment is both formative and summative. ***Formative assessment*** is ongoing throughout the teaching-learning process with checkpoints along the way, and ***summative assessment*** is the judgment of students' overall performance. During formative assessments, you are constantly seeking ways to teach and give feedback to students to improve their performance in learning and to improve your performance in teaching as well. Continuous formative and self-assessment of students combined with their ongoing dialog with you are very helpful in facilitating continuous student progress. ***Dialog assessment*** is two-way interaction between you and the students, wherein students give you their self-assessment of progress and you provide feedback to them on the accuracy their self-assessment. Formative assessment aids you and your students in making summative judgments about the quality of student performance at the end of the cycle of learning in the performance exhibition.

Assessment in this professional development series concerns the teaching and learning of essential knowledge and the formative and summative assessment of student learning through holistic demonstrations of their learning. In this regard, you must take care to assure that the process is not driven by fragments of learning or isolated skills and that the assessments do not predominate and take precedence over your role in teaching. *Instances abound where assessment focuses on the learning of minute skills or places the burden on the <u>student </u>to learn without the clear explicit teaching that makes it possible to meet assessment standards.* Instead, you must teach for important demonstrable outcomes, expect all students to learn and perform well, and you must provide the expertise in teaching to ensure excellence in students' learning and performances. The Culturally-Transformative Teaching Model in Volume IV explains in detail how this is done.

Authentic Assessment: the Three P's

The performance tasks include the 3 Ps of performance assessment: ***Portfolios, Projects***, and ***Performances.*** The portfolio is a compilation of representative samples of student written work, the project is usually a three-dimensional student-generated project or activity that takes place over a period of time, and the performance is an "on your feet" student presentation of accomplishment in a designated area of the curriculum.

Portfolios provide evidence of the quality of student written work in a variety of academic areas from week-to-week subject to subject. The portfolio, which shows student cumulative growth also serves as a source for discussion during parent conferences. At the secondary level, the portfolio takes on a more formal structure as student written work includes more structured essays. The topics selected for the essays are designed so that students discuss world-wide issues and understandings, service to school and community, and student reflections, perceptions, and self-assessments of their growth in understanding and contributing to the betterment of society.

Projects include subject-related models based on real-world tasks that lend themselves to enhancing cross-cultural understanding. The projects take the form of a product or process. They are generally developed over a longer expanse of time, require creativity, critical thinking, and problem solving and may be conducted cooperatively. At the early grades, projects may be as simple as the typical science project. At the secondary, however, projects may extend to conducting relevant research in the community and carrying out community service projects. Such projects can include written and oral presentations as assessment components, and when this occurs, each of the 3 P's are embraced as a single overarching assessment endeavor. This method is particularly appropriate at the secondary level where an integration and analysis of student intellectual development and cultural sensitivity can be set up and assessed as a requirement for graduation.

Performances are the highlight of authentic performance assessment. They require students to demonstrate, through an integrated "on your feet" performance, the content and process of their learning, in this case with parents and community members as the audience. In performance exhibitions, students demonstrate, with increasing levels of sophistication and formality, their growth both in subject matter concepts and skills and in cross-cultural development and understanding. The exhibitions may be individual or group oriented depending on the age and capability of the students. During the elementary grades, whole-class presentations are suggested, with each student contributing. At the upper elementary grades through high school, individual student performances take precedence over group performance. Just as the portfolio of written work takes on more formal structure at the secondary level, the performance is also more structured. As a graduation requirement students demonstrate their overall growth in learning through their performances before a panel of parents, teachers, and other school representatives. The performance exhibition is discussed further in *Module Two* as the highlight of learning, the medium for involving families in the learning of students throughout the year, and the culminating event of the year.

The performance exhibition, as outlined in this series, is the summative assessment of student performance as it is demonstrated at the end of the school year. It is used for you and others to make judgments about student progress. In the context of this professional development series, the students' cultural knowledge including the ways in which students are developing into culturally sensitive human beings is the ultimate gauge that you, your parents, and the students themselves use to determine how well you and the school are doing. The learning expectations define the standards, both cognitive and affective, which students are expected to demonstrate. Excellence in student learning means that the student is striving to demonstrate these qualities.

Other Methods of Measuring Student Performance

Even though authentic performance assessment is strongly supported in this series as the focal point of the curriculum, teaching, and student learning, there are other forms of assessment that you should know about and have in your repertoire as conventional measures of student learning. Standardized tests are forms of measurement that are supposedly objective. They are developed and administered under uniform conditions, and valued for their *reliability* in accurately measuring what they intend to measure, their efficiency, and their cost effectiveness in making comparisons among large groups of students. The two types of standardized tests are ***norm-referenced***, which compares the achievement of an identified group of students to a representative national sample and lets teachers and schools know how well their particular group of students compares with this national norm. ***Criterion-referenced tests*** are used to determine whether a student has mastered specific learning objectives according to a designated criterion. Criterion-referenced tests have great benefits for measuring specific student learning especially when they take the form of performance assessment to measure authentic student learning.

In this ***accountability*** era when teachers and schools are being called to account for student learning, ***high stakes testing*** is coloring much of what occurs in classrooms. These standardized mandated tests by which both students and educators are judged can have serious consequences. Students may be placed in special programs, retained, or judged ineligible for graduation. Teachers may lose salaries, advancement, or even their jobs. Schools and school districts may lose funding, staff, and ultimately their right to exist based on students' performance on the achievement tests. In addition to these problematic outcomes, a broad spectrum of the community continues to raise fundamental concerns about such high stakes testing. Standardized achievement tests, and intelligence tests in particular, continue to be questioned by cultural groups and educational authorities for their ***cultural bias***; that is, these tests measure student ability and achievement based on dominant-culture criteria and therefore may be biased against other cultures. Their concern is that the uses made of such tests can have severe and far-reaching consequences for non-dominant culture students. There also continues to be considerable debate among professional educators as well as among many citizens and policy makers about standardized testing in general. Professional educators generally oppose such testing while policy makers believe standardized testing is valuable and should be continued.

In spite of the issues and barriers, it is generally concluded that accountability systems which include high stakes tests will continue to prevail in schools and classrooms. Your use of *multiple measures,* including your own observations and judgments of student growth in learning is, in this series, the most highly recommended way to get an overall picture of student learning. Standardized tests have the least ***validity***, in the sense of obtaining a true measure of what a student knows. Authentic assessment is the most valid since the tasks are based on what students are learning from day to day in classrooms. Nonetheless, this era of accountability demands that students demonstrate that they have internalized the dominant "culture of power" by passing these high stakes "gateway" standardized tests. Thus, it is incumbent upon you to help students do well on these tests by becoming familiar with the types of tasks that students are asked to perform, and at a minimum, help students master the tasks called for on these high stakes tests. The students' futures in mainstream American culture depend on it.

A Curriculum to Develop World-Wide Perspectives and Cross-Cultural Understanding

The curriculum recommendations in this module are culturally-centered on obtaining world-wide perspectives which lead ultimately to emancipatory knowledge. Peter McLaren (2007) refers to *emancipatory knowledge* as knowledge aimed at creating the conditions under which irrationality, domination, and oppression are transformed in the interest of knowledge to serve all of the world's people. To be emancipatory, knowledge cannot be static, constraining or designed to foster a single point of view or cultural perspective. It must allow for freedom of thought where one point of view is juxtaposed against another with the aim of seeking truth. While the recommended course of study in this module has the aim of helping students achieve cross-cultural understanding, it is also emancipatory in that it is designed to emancipate or free students from the constraints of dominant-culture learning.

Expanding Curriculum for World-Wide Perspectives

What is to be taught and how it is to be taught has much to do with one's background knowledge and experiences. It is generally accepted that meaningful learning is based on new experiences that make sense to learners, experiences that are connected to the students' schema or background knowledge. Schema theory recognizes that learning is embedded in culture in this case both dominant and non-dominant cultures and therefore teaching and learning must acknowledge and build on the background knowledge of both cultures. A limited and limiting application of this "background knowledge" criterion is the "me to other" curriculum orientation of beginning with the *dominant-culture student's immediate surroundings* and expanding outward. This approach has become known as the ***expanding horizons curriculum*** or "local to global" view of curriculum. The expanding horizons approach is analyzed throughout this series because it is this curriculum theory, as discussed in earlier volumes, which governs much of the curriculum in American schools. It restricts American students in their ability to reach out and take on the perspectives of others throughout the world and it disregards the background knowledge and alternative perspectives of students from other cultures. Essentially, the expanding horizons doctrine is limited in its scope and it also discounts you, the teachers, who are the mediators of student learning through the curriculum. Your role is to broaden students' experiences by building a bridge from the known to the new; that is, to *build the necessary background knowledge* to assure students' understanding of new experiences.

Nel Noddings challenges the assumption behind the expanding horizons curriculum as well (Noddings 2000, 123). She agrees that the local can inform the global, but that the global can also inform the local, and that it is appropriate pedagogically to begin with distant events and then move to the local. The "me, family, community, state, nation" approach to curriculum in America, she believes, does not acknowledge students' imaginations. Wisely chosen stories set in foreign places and other times can give students historical and global knowledge that would not be possible under the "me first" dominant-culture perspective. As discussed previously, other cultures are more likely to think according to an "other first" perspective and consider themselves as one small part of the broader world. These cultures use the larger world as the context or bigger picture to serve as their reference point and basis for understanding the circumstances of distinct locales.

Critical pedagogy theorists, (Giroux 1988) and (McLaren 2007), shed light on ways that you can build cross-cultural understanding through your curriculum approach. McLaren believes that you need to know and actively teach the cultural and historical context surrounding the curriculum endeavors in the classroom which he says should provide students with the background and skills that are basic for analysis and leadership in the modern world. And, Giroux in particular, believes that as teachers, you are the intellectuals who should be given the autonomy to make such important curriculum decisions for your classroom.

Giroux also offers his insights to some "liberal" educators who have felt it necessary to eliminate "dominant and dominating curriculum and practices" from the schools. He believes that what is missing in their argument is a method and pedagogy for dealing with both dominant and non-dominant cultures. He calls for useful knowledge and classroom practice to emancipate subordinate groups by transforming power relations. Such a curriculum, he believes would include general skills of analysis, concepts, ideas, and principles rather than abstract content. It would take into account the historical and social particularities of the students as a starting point and be developed around knowledge forms that challenge and critically appropriate the ideology of the dominant culture rather than rejecting it outright (Giroux 1988 184-185).

This professional development series is in accord with the line of reasoning of Noddings, Giroux, and McLaren and consequently it is concerned with helping you investigate and position dominant-culture content so that it is part of a broader world-wide context. This viewpoint for handling dominant-culture content prevails throughout the culturally-centered education program, in the design of the curriculum and in the process of teaching it.

The Curriculum Approach

Jerome Bruner provides the background for the series' curriculum model. His theory is set forth in his 1960 classic, The Process of Education, which is concerned with the intellectual purposes of education. Bruner's concern is not simply with transmitting knowledge, but with the underlying structure of complex knowledge. The principle of knowledge transfer from one context to another, applicability of learning in multiple contexts, and the continual broadening and deepening of understanding in terms of basic and general ideas are at the heart of his theory. His interest is with *the structure of a discipline,* the pervasive and powerful ideas that are fundamental to a body of knowledge rather than isolated facts without context.

Bruner believes students' grasp of structure permits them to have a deep understanding of the essence of knowledge in a way that permits other things to be related to it. For example, students first learn the broad structure of a field of knowledge (world history) so they can relate other more specific content (U.S. history) to it. In this way, earlier and broader knowledge places later more specific knowledge in context by providing a bigger more general picture and relating what is learned later to things learned earlier. This emphasis on structure and a thorough grasp of general principles is valuable for all students. It is useful for dominant-culture students who typically are taught detailed "facts" from a dominant-culture perspective in isolation without regard to context, and for students from non-dominant cultures who may be thrown off track without the bigger picture to use as a reference point. Bruner believes that (1) the teaching of fundamental principles makes a subject more comprehensible (2) Unless detailed material is placed into a structured pattern, it is easily forgotten (3) Once a person learns the fundamental principles he or she has the grounding and a model for understanding other things like it, the essence of transfer.

Another of Bruner's theories that under girds this series' approach to curriculum delivery is that you can teach subject matter to any student by representing it in terms of the student's way of viewing things. The better you know the subject, the better you can shape and target it to students at different developmental levels and to students with different cultural backgrounds and experiences.

Subject Matter Recommendations to Promote Cross-Cultural Understanding

The subject matter recommendations presented in this section of the module embrace Bruner's work by emphasizing the structure of each recommended discipline, as a scientist or mathematician would, in the student's way of understanding. The direction and the points of emphasis in the seven recommended curriculum strands are intended to guide you in addressing the dominant "culture of power" phenomenon as you shape the

Eurocentric curriculum to broaden students' knowledge and understanding of cultures world-wide.

Following from Bruner's theory, that any subject can be learned successfully if it is presented in the student's way of viewing things, it is recommended that you keep ***Piaget's stages of intellectual development*** in the back of your mind, by beginning with the concrete and informal and then moving to the more abstract and formal, but you should not be constrained by the stages he proposes. It is also recommended that you avoid placing a ceiling on what students can learn or assigning an absolute level of difficulty to subject matter.

The descriptions which follow suggest the priorities of this professional development series in terms of recommended subject matter categories, general principles, and points for emphasis to be considered in a culturally-centered curriculum. The recommendations apply whether you are involved in *designing a new* culturally-centered education program or in *shaping an existing* dominant-culture curriculum toward world-wide perspectives.

World Cultures is as a multidisciplinary strand which combines the disciplines of history and geography to focus on the cultures of the world. This strand is designed to assure that American students are no longer naïve about what is going on in the world or where in the world it is going on. The aim is to have students learn about the world to balance and offset the western orientation of the typical American social studies curriculum—to have students know the truth about history and the people of the world through an accurate portrayal of their lives and institutions. It is recommended that history and geography be given great attention so that students learn the causes and consequences of people sharing this earth and the many factors that shape the past, present, and future. This understanding of the human condition worldwide, its common needs and common struggles, is essential for students to understand and have empathy with all cultures. It is recommended that history and geography be taught to younger students through stories and biographies of world citizens using the "Many years ago in a designated part of the world" approach. Points of comparison with national 21st century current events and distant and past events are recommended approaches to be used with upper grade students.

Communicative Arts (listening, speaking, reading, and writing) are the essence of literacy, and the ability to communicate in two or more languages is a high curriculum priority. The aim of the communicative arts curriculum strand is to develop effective communicators across cultures. As the most encompassing curriculum area, the communicative arts cross all subjects and are to be taught in ways that help students learn all of the subjects. The study of world cultures, for example, would provide much of the rich and meaningful content for students to listen to, talk, read, and write about. Similarly, the communicative arts processes would be used as tools to help students learn about world cultures and all other subject matter. They would help students learn to write compositions and creative stories and to understand the structure of sentences and paragraphs. In writing, they would encourage the flow of words and ideas through the direct and deliberate teaching of composition, the writing process, grammar, and spelling. Oral language experiences would concentrate on vocabulary, pronunciation, diction, grammar and fluency, and each time students are engaged in daily planned conversation, they would be encouraged to practice these elements of oral language.

__Oratory__, the practice of eloquent public speaking is recommended as a special component of the communicative arts curriculum strand. Through oratory, an area of literacy that has been under-developed in dominant-culture curriculum, students can learn the power of the spoken word and ways that public speaking can help them promote cross-cultural understanding in a powerful way. Oratory can also offer a unique opportunity for students to empathize with diverse cultures by learning about their communication patterns. Oratory challenges students to expand their cultural perspectives, to be more universal in thinking about language, and to consider some techniques that have been employed by orators of various cultures and backgrounds to influence their audiences. Obviously, performance exhibitions require students to be skilled in oratory. Even so, a special performance presentation in oral speaking and interpretation is also recommended as an annual culminating performance exhibition event.

In the process of teaching oral speaking, it is recommended that attention be given to the language strengths of linguistically diverse students. It is generally believed that African Americans, for example, value and excel in verbal adroitness, quick wit, and facility with metaphor and rhythm and rhyme as evident in the language use of the black preacher. It is also commonly recognized that Native Americans have a special talent for storytelling and saying a lot with few words. By emphasizing oratory all students, especially those from diverse groups such as these, would be taught to capitalize on and promote their strengths in oratory, and to share their oratorical skill with classmates, teachers, and members of the community.

__Additive Bilingualism__ as another component of the Communicative Arts curriculum strand is concerned with adding a new language rather than subtracting an existing language. It recognizes that speaking English in concert with other languages can make people stronger as individuals and as a society. You may wonder how you can effectively teach communicative arts if you are not fluent in the language of your students. It is generally believed now that fluency in a language is secondary to encouraging students to use their native languages and cultural knowledge as resources for learning. It is recommended that you support the language students bring to school, provide input in the new language, and let students use the new language in a non-threatening environment as constant correction may affect a student's attitude toward the new language.

Mathematics is recommended to be viewed as a way of thinking which emphasizes concepts, relationships, structures, and problem solving skills. As a goal it seeks to have students think, reason, and communicate as if they were mathematicians, often performing tasks such as measuring, estimating, and performing operations "in their heads," and to have students understand the relationship between mathematics and the real world. By teaching patterns and relationships, geometry and measurement, statistics and probability the recommendation is to assure that students have a sufficient background in the underpinnings of mathematics as it relates to cultures worldwide and as the basis for their success with mathematical processes in the more abstract attributes of algebra, geometry, and statistics. In the teaching of mathematics, skills and concepts would be introduced through simple terms and concrete materials and students would be encouraged to explain the strategies and reasoning they use to obtain solutions to problems. Both male and female students of all cultures would be taught to believe in themselves as learners of mathematics.

Life Sciences where the focus is on zoology, botany, and ecology are recommended as a curriculum strand in the culturally-centered education program. As part of this emphasis, students learn to think and behave as scientists by applying the scientific method to learn the nature of living systems. Students study a variety of plants and animals in their natural habitats and learn the interdependence of the ecosystem. Direct observation, participation, and action would require students to accept and carry out their responsibility for defending and improving the environment. It is recommended that an essential thrust of the life science program be environmental study to develop students' awareness and sensitivity to the environment, how it functions, how people interact within it, and how human actions affect the global ecosystem. Students would be encouraged to develop a ***global ethic*** which conforms to humanity's place in the universe. The global ethic sees nature's processes and life support systems as entitled to respect, not exploitation, by some human beings at the expense of other human and living things. This ecological thrust is integral to the study of the world and its cultures. It is recommended, therefore, that each student be required to complete an actual life science project involving action and reflection.

The Arts are expressions of the essence of humanity and therefore it is recommended that this discipline be strongly emphasized. In this strand of the curriculum students would be given the opportunity to gain broad knowledge of the arts of the world's peoples including their music, art, and dance and they would have the opportunity to study and practice selected arts in depth. Students would also be given the opportunity to appreciate the work of artists throughout the world and to participate in and produce works of art which enable them to see how culture is represented among the artifacts of the world's peoples. Artists from the community and beyond would be invited to perform and students would take trips to the theater, symphony, art museum, and community functions to be part of the creative contributions of the world's artists. The arts would also be an integral part of the school environment. Paintings of the world's artists would appear on classroom walls and hallways, and world music from all of the continents would be played in a variety of forms throughout the day and used in a variety of ways to create mood and effect.

Health and Physical Well Being as a strand of the curriculum develops the necessary knowledge and habits for a lifetime of health and well-being. Along with learning about the American lifestyle and diet, students would learn to appreciate different foods, forms of exercise, and the ways in which lifestyle plays a part in health and disease prevention in this country and in other parts of the world. They also would learn about movement and dance, sports and athletes, and the unique ways in which physical activity contributes to the lives of people throughout the world.

Community Service is recommended as a strand of the curriculum to take place throughout the grades. In the early grades, students would seek ways to learn about and provide help to the community. At the secondary level, students would design and carry out a community service project in which they give of themselves to help others. The community service project would be an outgrowth of the student's analysis and understanding of issues within the community. From their study, interactions, and discussions with community members, students can formulate their own beliefs and then put them into action. From designing and carrying out such a long-term project, students can learn about ways to address some of the oppression and inequity faced by many people in the community. Community service projects set the stage for students to also consider ways in which they can contribute to the lives and well-being of others in this country and abroad.

The Teacher Read-Aloud: An Essential Resource for Building Cross-Cultural Understanding

World and multicultural literature can be very powerful in shaping students' attitudes and regard for the world's peoples and for addressing issues that are inherent in living together in a multicultural society. Katie Wood Ray (1999) shares her ideas in her intensive discussion of the value and use of the read aloud. Her discussion makes it clear that that there is nothing more profound and conducive to fostering positive attitudes and building a cross-cultural classroom community than having the poignant and relevant literature of other cultures and far-away places read aloud to students on a daily basis. The messages conveyed through the daily reading can cause the class-as-a-whole to take on qualities expressed in these literary works.

Following are attributes which convey the power of the read aloud and ways that you can make the reading aloud of multicultural literature the essential academic routine of your daily classroom practice agenda. *It is recommended that you begin each class session with a multicultural read-aloud. Then, you can expand on the multicultural reading in other activities throughout the day or session.*

When you read-aloud, the knowledge and insights you provide about distant worlds—places and ways of doing things—move students into world cultures beyond their day-to-day dominant-culture studies. In the same way, the fluency of the text and the sound of your voice provide a model for students who are learning Standard English. When you make the commitment to read aloud to your students on a daily basis, the results for students of all cultures are immeasurable. You are giving your students information and insights that are seldom expressed in traditional textbooks, you are presenting it in an interesting and dynamic way that fully engages students, and you are providing an effective model of language: word pronunciation, fluency, phrasing, intonation, and grammar.

The Read-Aloud can set the stage for building cross-cultural understanding for all grade levels, kindergarten through adult levels. In fact, it is not uncommon for professors at the university level, or other adult educators, who like me, begin their course sessions by reading a relevant fiction or non-fiction literary selection aloud. To have impact, however, you need to have a plan for delivering high-quality multicultural literature to students. This requires more than simply picking up a book and reading it to the class. It is most effective when you establish the multicultural read-aloud as the academic routine, use it for instructional purposes to set the stage for the day or session, and are committed to use it as a consistent forum for developing cross-cultural understanding. Your use of the Read-Aloud for this purpose, however, calls for special skills and qualities. There are some key points for you to consider in setting up a comprehensive plan for delivering multicultural literature to students through the read-aloud.

First, it is important for you to know and emphasize to your students that the read-aloud can bring: shared characters, shared language, and shared journeys to your room.

- The read-aloud puts new people in the classroom. In a room where the read-aloud is a powerful force, the characters actually live in the room with you. Students come to love and care for the characters. What happens to the characters in the reading really matters to the students.

- The read-aloud gives you and your students a new language to speak while you are together, an insider's language in which you actually use words and phrases from the reading to describe actual events taking place in the classroom.

- The read-aloud allows you and your students to inhabit parallel worlds together. You and your students are able to live in your every-day world and live in the world of the book at the same time. During the class session, you and students' minds will often slip into the world of the book that you are reading. You may be experiencing the splendor of the orient, the adventure of an African safari, or the hardship of a slave plantation. As Dr. Seuss would say "Oh, the places you can go!" Nothing else that you do during the day quite matches the new worlds that bring you and your students together. It's how you and your students become a community!

Second, it is important for you to know that there are better ways than others to share read-aloud time. For your read-aloud to have impact, you need to plan for its success. Your preparations should include at least the following: time, expectations, reading aloud well, and getting your students to believe in you.

- Try to schedule ten to twenty minutes at the start of the class session so that the read- aloud can serve as the catalyst for what is to come. And in addition to this regular time, try other times before or after lunch or recess, or at the end of the class session. Also, get students to read similar books on their own.

- Expect students to listen attentively and then apply the reading concepts to build cross-cultural understanding in the classroom. To direct their listening give them three points to listen for, encourage them to listen fully without interrupting, and then later you can hold a discussion and encourage follow up activities related to the reading.

- Recognize your reading aloud as a sound that stands out from all of the other sounds in the room. You need to make a space for the read-aloud. Practice so that you know the texts that you read aloud inside out before you read them aloud to students. Insist on *perfect attention* from every student, no paper rattling, etc. Take time, a few moments of silence and make eye contact with students before you begin, and leave your teaching voice, student reprimands, etc. at the edge of the carpet.

  Be dramatic. Honor the sound and the absence of sound. Read slowly, making pauses when it feels right to do so, and hold the silence at the end.

- Make sure that your students believe in you; they must feel that you care about what you are reading to them—that you truly care about the words you are reading to them, that you care about the characters, and that you care about the journey and time frame that you share together. You must give your students the feeling that you are reading, not only because it's good for them, but that it's good for you as well. In other words, you must convey that read aloud time is very "special time" that you and your students spend together.

  Third, it is important for you to have a repertoire of books on multicultural topics to read to students in a balanced way to address specific needs and interests. Multicultural books such as the following sample from Children's Literature: An Invitation to the World by Diana Mitchell (2003) and Multicultural Education of Children and Adolescents by Baruth & Manning (2004) are considerations:

Native Americans

SkySisters, by Jan Bourdeau Waboose
Rain Is Not My Indian Name, by Cynthia Leitich Smith
The Good Luck Cat, by Joy Harjo
The Unbreakable Code, by Sara Hoagland Hunter
Jingle Dancer, by Cynthia Leitich Smith
To Live in Two Worlds: American Youth Today, by Brent Ashabranner
The Desert is Theirs, by Byrd Baylor
The Talking Earth, by Jean Craighead George

African Americans

Bippity Bop Barbership, by Natasha Anastasia Tarpley
M.C. Higgins the Great, by Virginia Hamilton
Dinner at Aunt Connie's House, by Faith Ringgold
Uptown, by Bryan Collier
Scorpions, by Walter Dean Myers
Breaking the Chain: African American Slave Resistance. By William Loren Katz
Roll of Thunder, Hear My Cry, by Mildred D. Taylor

Latin Americans

Tomas and the Library Lady, by Pat Mora
Salsa Stories, by Lulu Delacre
Snapshots from the Wedding, by Gary Soto
In My Family/En mi familia, by Carmen Lomas Garza
Crazy Loco, by David Rice
Central America and the Panama, by Patricia Markun
And Now Miguel, by Joseph Krumgold

Asian Americans

Child of the Owl, by Laurence Yep
Yang the Third and Her Impossible Family, by Lensey Namioka
Finding My Voice, by Marie G. Lee
A Step from Heaven, by An Na
The Trip Back Home, by Janet S. Wong

Behind Barbed Wire: The Imprisonment of Japanese Americans During World War II, by Daniel Davis
The Serpent's Children, by Laurence Yep

Arab/Muslim Americans

The Egyptian Cinderella, by Shirley Climo
The Golden Sandal: A Middle Eastern Cinderella Story, by Rebecca Hickox
Children of Israel, Children of Palestine, by Laurel Holliday
The Rise of Islam, by John Child
Ramadan, by Suhaib Hamid Ghazi
What Do We Know About Islam, by Shahrukh Husain

International Characters

The Breadwinner, by Deborah Ellis
Sitti's Secret, by Naomi Shihab Nye
The Other Side of Truth, by Beverley Naidoo
The Color of My Words, by Lynn Joseph
Samir and Yonatan by Daniella Carmi

New Voices in Historical Fiction

Dragon's Gate, by Laurence Yep
Nim and the War Effort, by Milly Lee
The Birchbark House, by Louise Erdrich
The Land, by Mildred D. Taylor
Voices of the Alamo, by Sherry Garland

Race or Social Class Issues

The Other Side, by Jacqueline Woodson
Bat 6, by Virginia Euwer Wolff
Esperanza Rising, by Pam Munoz Ryan
The Heart of a Chief, by Joseph Bruchac
Witness, by Haren Hesse

Using multicultural books to read aloud brings up the issue of bias and stereotypes. The major question is whether you should use or exclude books which convey bias and stereotypes. In accord with the approach taken throughout the series relative to the complicated issue of teaching dominant culture content, the response is "Yes!" It doesn't stop there, however. Obviously, you should select pieces of literature that will invite your students in, and not alienate or make them uncomfortable. Yet, in keeping with the recommendation by Giroux to critically appropriate the dominant culture in other instances, when you use such books for instructional purposes, you have the special opportunity to teach students about bias and stereotypes and open up these areas for discussion. For example, when a holiday such as Christmas is discussed as an American tradition, you are in a position to clarify and broaden the text presentation by explaining that other countries also celebrate Christmas and that comparable traditions exist in other cultures. Similarly, when African American characters are depicted in selections as maids for example, you have the opportunity to elevate the discussion by examining the concept of servitude historically and from multiple perspectives. Such discussions can emphasize how people other than African Americans have taken on roles as servants and even today continue to serve in such roles. As you can see, like other dominant-culture material, when used effectively in a manner which conveys your cultural competence, the read aloud can be a very significant instructional tool for challenging and broadening students' perspectives.

In addition to broadening students' cultural horizons and their skill in listening and through the read-aloud, you can also use it to help students learn to speak Standard English. Extensions of the read-aloud for this purpose may include activities for students to learn and grow in their expressive language abilities through chanting, imitating, storytelling and reciting, holding conversations and discussions about the reading, and retelling the selection by responding in complete sentences. Standard English is modeled and facilitated on a daily basis through these activities.

For all students, perhaps the most important and lasting parallel to the teacher read-aloud is the student read-aloud. Certainly, each day as you read aloud, students have a model to emulate as an inspiration for their own oral expression with text. The ability to read aloud well is an important literacy skill to be developed routinely and regularly in a culturally-centered education program as part of daily classroom practice. Students are ready to read aloud well and share passages with others, however, only after they have read the selection silently, become familiar with it, and practiced reading it orally until they are comfortable sharing it with others. In other words, careful preparation is essential.

In the culturally-centered education program, students' facility with oral reading is assessed at regular intervals, developed during the year through daily practice in the classroom and at home, and demonstrated in the end-of-year performance exhibitions. In the process, care is taken to develop students' self-concepts through success experiences, compliments, and recognitions. As a companion to this module, the MASS Professional Development Series offers as a supplement to enhancing the communicative arts curriculum "The Culturally-Centered Integrated Literacy Classroom," which presents a model and explains in detail how to set up and implement a language-based culturally-centered classroom for grades K-8.

Structuring the Education Program

The formal curriculum, the official curriculum of the school or district, drives much of what goes on in classrooms. Long range, mid-range, and short range planning are essential if students are to demonstrate the level of achievement outlined in the curriculum. In the context of the culturally-centered education program of this professional development series, the curriculum would spell out the benchmarks, the knowledge and behaviors students are expected to demonstrate in performance exhibitions. In this sense, you engage in backward planning, beginning with the end in mind, planning for what you expect students to demonstrate at the end of the year. For example, students would exhibit through **declarative knowledge**, *what they know* about something, through **procedural knowledge** they demonstrate *what they are able to do*, and through **conditional knowledge** they convey what they *know, can do, and when and how to apply what they know and can do.* The performance exhibitions require students to demonstrate proficiency with these forms of knowledge. You therefore need to plan the curriculum to enable students to demonstrate competency in these knowledge forms and behaviors in an ongoing manner throughout the year, and at the end of the year in the performance exhibitions.

Most school districts provide a **curriculum guide,** which includes a scope and sequence of the subjects to be taught at each grade level. In more and more school districts states are providing a mandated curriculum which also designates how subjects are to be taught; however, even in these situations most guides provide some discretion for the classroom teacher, grade level or school team to make some modifications. In this instance, your job is to take the mandated curriculum and shape its qualities so that it (1) is culturally-centered with a world-wide international focus, (2) calls for in-depth learning of essential knowledge, (3) has affective as well as cognitive dimensions, (4) views content from multiple perspectives, and (5) is concerned with the application of the knowledge and skills. The suggestions in this module and the module to follow are designed to help you do this effectively.

Long-Range Planning

Through **long-range planning** you specify in a general way the areas of focus for the entire school year to assure that the expected knowledge and skills are demonstrated in the performance exhibition at the end of the year. In the process of long-range planning you lay out the subject matter in the order that you think it should be taught, the time required, and the resources needed. You determine how many weeks, days, or hours are available to implement the curriculum, taking into account holidays, vacations, etc. A helpful way to do this is to take a roll of shelf paper, divide it into four sections to represent the four quarters of the school year, and briefly sketch out the subjects and your teaching plan for each quarter. When you think of the school year as apportioned in quarters, it helps you to see that you cannot simply plow ahead, one subject after another without reflection, but must take stock of where you are and the extent of student progress that is being made at the end of each quarter. It allows you to conduct quarterly assessments (interim performance exhibitions) on the learning tasks at the end of each quarter before moving on. The four-part approach to dividing up the school year is also expedient because student and parent motivation are high during quarterly assessment and reporting periods (with parent conferences and report card distribution) in most school districts held each quarter. Through this long-range planning approach you are building in assessments as you lay out the curriculum for the year.

Mid-Range or Unit Planning

Mid-range or unit planning breaks the long range plan into chunks or units often with a particular theme. You have an opportunity through the units that you develop to specify in more detail what and how students learn the material. In unit planning, you take the mandated curriculum and adapt it in ways that make it your own. Long-range plans provide the road map and mid-range plans make the content interesting and real. Through mid-range or unit planning, you have the best opportunity to build cross-cultural understanding through the curriculum and subject matter that you are required to teach. For example, when you design a thematic unit you can build in lessons to focus on particular cultural issues and shape student learning in the interest of emancipatory knowledge and cross-cultural understanding. The lessons which flow from the unit can be planned to have students take multiple perspectives on issues, ponder the results of taking one course of action over another, and consider the implications of what they are learning. This level of planning tends to be the most exciting because you get to display your own creativity and represent subject matter in ways that interest you. Your enthusiasm will most assuredly prompt student interest as well.

Caution about mid-range or unit planning and implementation is advised, however, since many curriculum theorists and developers are now using the unit as the segment of the curriculum from which they expect students to engage in learning activities and be assessed on what they have learned. When the focus is on the unit as the instructional entity and students are left to learn on their own, accountability for student learning is on the student rather than the teacher. Direct teaching of essential knowledge and processes can be nonexistent or even discouraged and, as a consequence, students fail to obtain the insights that can build cross-cultural understanding and excellence in learning. When learning is left to the students, and when students "fall through the cracks" teachers are never quite sure what happened, where the students got "off-track" in the learning progression. Learning segments can be organized in interesting and powerful ways around a unit theme, but this does not preclude planning and teaching well-defined lessons to assure that students learn the essential "big ideas" to accomplish the goals of the unit. The unit is the larger source from which the smaller well-crafted lesson is to be designed and taught.

Short-Range Planning

When you move from long range to mid-range to short range plans, you become more detailed in your thinking about content and skill development. You can think of *short-range planning* in three stages, the weekly plan that you may be required to write in your lesson plan book, the daily or session plan that you write on a chart or instructional board each day in the form of a daily or session agenda, and the plan for teaching the lesson, also written on a chart or instructional board in the form of a lesson agenda.

Weekly plans certainly make sense because they help you to realize that, if there are 52 weeks in a school year, you have a 52 week time parameter in which to achieve your instructional goals. Each of the weeks during the year is an opportunity for you to achieve something substantial with your class. When you make the announcement, "This week we will accomplish… you set in the minds of students what is expected during this time frame, and if you also announce at the end of the week, we accomplished… students are reminded that their efforts are paying off and are leading to something. Students, parents, and administrators think in terms of weekly plans and accomplishments; therefore, it can be useful to design your instructional program to complete certain tasks and accomplish certain goals in weekly segments. School principals are focused on what you do from week to week to such an extent that weekly planning is mandatory in many schools. Publishers print weekly lesson plan books, which many administrators purchase and distribute to each teacher, expecting them to be completed each Friday before the upcoming week. Some administrators even collect the weekly plans to assure that adequate teaching plans have been made for the week to come.

The day or session agenda is the weekly five-day plan broken down into daily segments. When you follow the agenda for the day or session consistently it becomes a routine structure for engaging students in learning. This level of planning as presented in Volume II in the form of the day or session agenda is a useful planning device and also an essential classroom management tool. Once the agenda of activities for the day or session is on the instructional board and presented orally to students, it becomes their plan as well. There is clarity in students' minds of events to come and your expectation for accomplishment. Students can then carry out their role in working with you be successful.

The lesson is referred to in this series as the micro level of planning and teaching and includes the lesson plan and lesson agenda. The lesson agenda sets up the lesson for the students by identifying the question to be answered in the lesson and by outlining the approach that you will take in teaching the lesson to enable them to answer the question. Teaching is the heart of the matter in student learning; it is the process that you engage in from day to day to achieve the desired outcome of your plans. Culturally transformative teaching, spelled out in Volume IV, sets forth a comprehensive, systematic process that you should master to teach effectively to build cross-cultural understanding and assure excellence in student learning.

The five types of plans described in this module are the essential tools for shaping curriculum "in process" to build cross-cultural understanding. The discussion of long-term, mid-term, and short-term planning suggests the level and quality of thinking that is needed. The planning process becomes a worthy undertaking when you realize that by taking the extensive time that it takes to set up the educational program according to the types of plans described, you are learning the process of curriculum planning as a road map for your teaching, a skill that will last over a lifetime of teaching. Each year as you carry out your plans, you can make them more refined. Curriculum planning is extensive and challenging initially but it becomes easier each successive year. The typical concern that you may have though, particularly if you are a new teacher, is how to begin. As with other complex tasks, it is necessary to predict or project your plans, and make modifications along the way until you have a feel for the learning tasks, the students, the time allocation, and the skill that you bring to the undertaking. Working with a curriculum planning consultant can help you and your colleagues get started and develop your skill in designing, planning and implementing a culturally-centered education program.

In this module, the diverse group of practicing classroom teachers was asked to discuss the culturally-centered educational program, its relationship to classroom practice and cross-cultural understanding, and to explain how they would adapt their current curriculum to address diverse cultures and build cross-cultural understanding. The discussion proceeded accordingly:

Classroom Teachers Talk It Over

"The first thing I can do to address diverse cultures is to present the material in various ways—visually, auditory, kinesthetic, and in the process improve their understanding. Second, as I present the material, I can also explain to students that there are many ways to complete the same task just as there are many kinds of people. Third, I can remind my students that we should applaud each other for our successes and help each other if we are struggling. These three approaches to learning can help to build cross-cultural understanding."

"Making my classroom curriculum field dependent, holistic and embedded in context can help my students, not only understand the material better, but also bring real life and education together. If we can understand our students and balance field dependent curriculum with content based details and analysis, the learning outcome would really be desirable and pleasing. Also Bruner's idea of teaching the fundamental principles of a subject making it more comprehensible takes us back to field dependent, close to the real world."

"Effective teaching is necessarily concerned with the teacher's flexibility and adaptability. Although the formal curriculum may not explicitly address diversity and cross-cultural understanding, I believe that I should be willing to go beyond the "requirements" to address topics of importance. I can encourage my students to consider other's views and begin perspective-taking practices by presenting many views about topics that consider the thoughts and views of others as valuable, and I can provide ample opportunities for students to see and be part of other cultural practices in authentic settings. For me learning is much more than complying with a rigid set of state and national standards. It is truly about understanding the broad spectrum of students in my classroom and adapting what I teach to best meet their needs."

"The best way to adapt my current curriculum would be to expand it to embrace a world-wide perspective. Expanding the curriculum to focus on world history, instead of only on U.S. history is an appropriate place to start. By not limiting our young students to the ideas of "me, family, community, state, country" we are fostering their global view which increases cross-cultural understanding. Including general and fundamental skills rather than abstract ones and focusing on analysis of concepts, ideas, and principles foster strength and leadership in our modern world."

As you conclude this module, consider the views of these classroom managers and be prepared to give your view? How do your thoughts about the educational program compare with the views expressed by these classroom managers?

Summary of Module One

This module has focused on discussing and presenting strategies for setting up your education program to build cross-cultural understanding. The curriculum and subject matter proposed in this module incorporate the ideas of (Bruner 1960), (Giroux 1988), and (McLaren 2007) in their proposals for a curriculum to produce students who are culturally literate and socially responsible. What students learn, and the way in which they learn it, are of major concern in building cross-cultural understanding. In this module of the professional development series, the culturally-centered education program is essentially concerned with curriculum (what is taught), and the results (the assessment) in terms of student performance of authentic tasks. The teaching process (how it is taught) is discussed in Volume IV. Some recommendations regarding key areas of the curriculum, the performance exhibition, and the recommended subject matter are offered to guide you as you begin to consider how you will set up your culturally-centered education program. The adaptations that you make to the district curriculum should shape it in a culturally-centered coherent way using the culturally-referenced priorities of this module. The adaptations are those which you can make yourself, with a team of colleagues, or working with a consultant.

This module begins by explaining how to get to know students—their backgrounds and indications about how they learn. It continues with explaining the performance exhibition as the focus of student learning, areas of emphasis and adaptations to the curriculum that you can make to create a culturally-centered education program, and ways to plan for it to happen. In review, some specific points are:

- The module explained how a culturally-centered education program supports classroom practice to build cross-cultural understanding. The recommendation is to address the curriculum priorities identified in this module, and to ascertain and build on knowledge of cultural groups and individuals wherever appropriate so that you can also incorporate that knowledge into the educational program as well.

- The multiple ways that students learn and strategies that you can employ to promote learning and build cross-cultural understanding have been discussed in this module. Special emphasis was placed on cognitive style and a variety of other methods to accommodate student diversity in learning.

- Student exhibitions of learning and ways to make student performance the centerpiece of your educational program have been explained. The ways in which end of year exhibitions serve as the target of instruction are outlined in this module. The actual detail of performance assessment and how the performances include families and community members will be spelled out later in Module Two of this volume.

- The module has provided insights into ways to adapt the curriculum to foster multiple cultural perspectives. Some specific examples for ways in which a variety of subject matter areas can be shaped to promote world-wide perspectives and cross-cultural understanding have been suggested. Reading aloud multicultural books were strongly recommended to serve as the focal point of your daily academic routine to build cross-cultural understanding. Multicultural fiction and non-fiction books and stories, when read aloud by teachers, can be a very powerful means to teach students about distant, historical, and current topics affecting cross-cultural understanding.

- The module has offered practical suggestions for focusing and structuring a culturally-centered education program in long and short-term ways. The long-term goal is to enable students to demonstrate academic proficiency and cross-cultural understanding during the year and in end of year performance exhibitions.

In the next module, you will learn ways to develop school-family relationships, and a process for working with families as a resource, ally, and source of support for promoting student learning and for building cross-cultural understanding.

Opening Scenario (Afterthoughts)

How would you assess the Curriculum approach used by the teacher after studying this module? Please explain. Would you use a similar approach in your classroom?

Questions/Activities

1. In what ways is a culturally-centered education program a support to classroom practice and a resource for cross-cultural understanding? What are some implications does this have for you as you begin to plan how you will operate your classroom?

2. What have you learned about how students learn, about cognitive style in particular, that can help you develop the learning abilities of all of your students

3. Explain the value of authentic assessment for assessing the learning of culturally-diverse students. How can you make performance assessment the focal point of learning in your classroom?

4. Explain the following concepts in relationship to the history of the dominant mainstream culture in America:

> Expanding horizons curriculum   high status principle
> cognitive style

5. How would you adapt the typical Eurocentric curriculum to foster diverse perspectives in ways that promote cross-cultural understanding?

6. Summarize the new ideas, principles, and concepts that you learned in this module and explain how you will implement the new insights in your classroom.

> Cooperative Group Activity:
>
> Students, working in small groups, take an area of their curriculum, such as social studies, and explain how they would use the module's subject matter recommendations to modify/complement their mandated curriculum.

Looking in Classrooms

Visit a classroom in your area for the purpose of finding out about the curriculum and assessment techniques used—in relationship to what you have learned in this module. Observe and note the following. (Ask questions of the teacher in areas in areas where you need clarification):

- Describe the educational program in the school/classroom. To what extent does the curriculum embrace all cultures?

- What strategies does the teacher use to implement the curriculum? How successful are students in learning the content and skills outlined in the curriculum? How do you know?

Following your visitation, write a <u>Brief Summary Statement</u> to explain what you observed in this setting and what you would do in your educational program to enhance cross-cultural understanding.

Recommendations for Further Reading

Marzano, R.J., D.J. Pickering, and J. McTighe. *Assessing Student Outcomes: Performance Assessment Using the Dimensions of Learning Model.* McREL Institute. Aurora, CO, 1993.

> This book provides a model of learning through performance assessment. It is compatible with the approach used in this textbook.

Helms, J. "Why Is There No Study of Cultural Equivalence in Standardized Cognitive Ability Testing?" *American Psychologist.* 47, 9, (1992): 1083-1101.

> This article discusses the issues and problems with intelligence tests. It is useful to understand cultural bias in measuring student ability.

Rowe, Mary Budd. "Wait Time, Slowing Down May be a Way of Speeding Up." *American Educator* 11, (Spring 1987): 38-43, 47.

> The use of "wait time" in teacher student interactions is one of the culturally-sensitive strategies that has been used effectively in classrooms. The learning gains and advantages of using "wait time" are pointed out in this article.

Wiggins, Grant. "Practicing What We Preach in Designing Authentic Assessment." *Educational Leadership* 54, 4 (1996-1997): 18-25.

> Grant Wiggins is widely recognized as the authority of authentic assessment. In this article, he challenges educators to stay on course with the concept. This textbook builds on Wiggins recommendations.

Bruner, Jerome S. *The Process of Education.* Cambridge Mass.: Harvard University Press, 1963.

> This book is a classic in the field. The basic principles to Bruner's curriculum theory are incorporated in this chapter of the textbook.

Module Two

Engaging Families as Partners in the Culturally-Centered Education Program

Opening Scenario...42

Key Concepts...44

<u>Topics Covered in This Module:</u>

- How a Supportive Relationship with Families Enhances Classroom Practice and Builds Cross-Cultural Understanding...44

- Cross-Cultural Communication: Concepts and Processes...46

    The Communication Process...46

    The Cross-Cultural Communication Process...47

    Listening, the Heart of Effective Communication...47

    Special Points for Communicating with Families...48

- Building Home-School Connections...49

    Making Schools More Like Homes and Homes More Like Schools...50

    The Classroom and Home as a Continuum of Learning...51

- A Range of Home-School Communication Techniques...52

    Two-Way Communication...53

        A Special Class for Parents...53
        An Open Door Policy...54
        Early Communication...54
        Telephone Calls...55
        Home Visits...55

       Special Recognitions—Families of the Week…55
       Conferences…56

   One-Way Communication…56

       Newsletters…57
       Student Work Samples…57
       Newspapers and Year Books…57
       Handbooks…58
       Media Sources and Presentations…58
       Email, Notes, and Letters…58

- Family Participation in Classroom Learning Events…59

       Back to School Family Orientations…59
       Open House…59
       The Performance Exhibitions…60

- Working with Families as Volunteers…60

       Volunteers to Share Their Talents…61
       Volunteers to Handle Book Publishing…61
       Volunteers as Classroom Tutors…61
       Volunteers to Host Special Days and Events…62

- The Performance Exhibition: A Ten-Step Process for Involving Families with Their Children in Learning…62

   1. Set the Stage for the Process in an Introductory Letter…63
   2. Initiate the Process at Back-to-School Orientation…63
   3. Chart the Course in Goal-Setting Conferences…64
   4. Use Newsletters to Motivate and Keep Families on Track…65
   5. Send Illustrative Student Work Samples Home Weekly…65
   6. Set Up Student-Family Projects…65
   7. Display Student Work at Open House…66
   8. Communicate Progress toward Exhibitions on Conference Day…66
   9. Conduct Monthly Interim Performance Exhibitions…66
 10. Put it All Together in End of Year Performance Exhibitions…67

Classroom Teachers Talk It Over…67

Summary of Module Two…68

Opening Scenario (Afterthoughts)…69

Questions/Activities…69

Looking in Classrooms…70

Recommendations for Further Reading…71

Opening Scenario

The challenge for community leaders in a small mid-western town is attempting to come to terms with the age-old problem in similar communities throughout America—How to get students and parents of color, who have been turned off to school become motivated and see value in school as a helpful and meaningful contributor to their lives. Even though most parents have tried to influence their children, the number of students who are apathetic about learning, truant, and dropping out of school has reached monumental proportions.

Since neither parents nor school officials have been unable to stem the tide, community members convinced that something must be done, are beginning to take responsibility and tackle the situation themselves. Some of the strategies they have considered are: working with teachers and principals to identify the source of the problem; calling on parents to urge them to have their children realize the significance of schooling to living a productive life in America; calling on the ministers of the various churches to counsel students; and making contact with officials in the judicial system to ask them to intervene with stiffer penalties for truancy.

Why do you think the students have become turned off to school? What challenges does this pose for school officials? What challenges does this pose for the students, their families, and the community?

Do the approaches used by community members seem appropriate and effective?

What perceptions do you have about working with families as you begin this module?

As you prepare to become or continue your role as a teacher in today's world of culturally diverse classrooms, you may or may not be able to identify with this situation. And you may also be wondering how in your role as classroom teacher you can contribute and improve conditions in a community such as this.

What can you do to restore faith in school for students and parents of color in communities across the country? The essential response is to make every effort to reach out to families of students proactively *before* they are "turned off" to school. The extent to which you are effective with families and the community is directly related to the quality of the educational program and the level, quality and extent of your communication with them.

Communication with families in relationship to the education program is emphasized in this module. Your effectiveness with families and others in the community begins with *their* perceptions of your competence in this area. Families and members of the community see your role as operating an effective educational program that embraces their culture and values. What and how well their sons and daughters are learning in your classroom is of paramount interest to them. If they feel that their child is learning in a manner that is compatible with their values and standards, if you communicate with them often in an ongoing manner, and if they are given a role to play in their child's education, the stage is set for a productive educational experience. Even at the secondary level students' and parents' attitudes toward school are affected by their perceptions of the quality of education that students are receiving and the extent and quality of the communication they receive from you.

In this module, you should focus on answering the following key questions:

- How can supportive family relationships enhance classroom practice and build cross-cultural understanding?

- What is cross-cultural communication, what are the processes involved, and what are some effective techniques to employ?

- What are some ways to create a continuum of learning through effective home-school connections?

- What kind of communication techniques can you employ to be effective in your work with families?

- How can you implement The Performance Exhibition: A Ten-Step Process for Involving Families the Learning of Their Children?

Key Concepts

encoding ~ student work samples ~ decoding ~ noise ~ beginning with the end in mind ~ intercultural communication ~ back-to-school family orientation ~ Eastern cultures ~ introductory letter ~ Performance Exhibition ~ Two-way communication ~ One-way communication

How a Supportive Relationship with Families Enhances Classroom Practice and Builds Cross-Cultural Understanding

One of the apprehensions that you can experience in culturally-diverse classrooms is how to work with families whose cultural backgrounds may differ from your own, and who may operate under a different lifestyle and approach to child rearing than you are accustomed to. If you, like many teachers, already have considerable consternation regarding your role in working with parents in general, adding the cultural dimension can only compound the feeling. There are some steps that you can take, however, to alleviate these worries and build supportive relationships with families.

Getting to know your families including some potential differences that may exist between families of dominant and non-dominant cultures, can help you begin to build high quality relationships with families. Many cultures have powerful family structures and qualities, which for the most part, are not typical of the traditional mainstream American view. One very important area for you to be aware of is that typically their commitment to family obligations and the collective betterment of the family take priority over individual motivation. Consequently, there may be discord if these families believe that American schools are intent on changing the belief system and cultural identity of students from culturally different groups to such an extent that the student's Americanized identity is in conflict with that of the family. Native Americans are one such group. They revere the elderly and believe that with age comes wisdom. The extended family, including grandparents, is important in a young person's home life and therefore important to include in the young person's school life. Similarly, it is the strength of the African American family which includes a strong religious, work, achievement, and upward mobility orientation that have served them well under the adverse conditions of slavery and segregation. You are also likely to find Asian families who have high aspirations for their children, a reverence for ancestors, and a respect for elderly persons. Latin Americans have equally strong family ties and many of the same extended family qualities represented among many non-dominant cultural groups.

Cultural competence and sensitivity are qualities that you need to convey as you seek to build positive relations with the families who are represented among the five cultural groups that we follow throughout the series. These qualities include taking great care not to make generalizations based upon limited information about a cultural group or individuals within the groups. In each cultural group, you will find both wealthy and poor families and highly educated scholars as well as unskilled workers. Similarly, it would be important to know whether the families have lived in the United States for 20 to 30 years or whether they are new arrivals for, the longer the families are here, the more Americanized and sophisticated they are likely to be in traversing the terrain of American schools. Most useful in building supportive relationships with families is to concentrate on cultural distinctions that may bear on the home-school relationship. In particular, it would be helpful in terms of building supportive relations with families to know that some non-dominant culture families may be reluctant to become actively involved in their children's schooling as they may view such involvement as an improper challenge to the authority of the teacher and school.

Your recognition and support of family relationships that differ from mainstream American family structures can enhance cross-cultural understanding in your classroom and in the broader community. Obviously, the goal of improving classroom practice through a culturally-centered education program calls for knowing and engaging with students' families. Your commitment to structure families' meaningful participation in the classroom's educational program and to provide frequent ongoing communication with them sets the stage for enhancing mutual respect and cross-cultural understanding. In this module, you will gain further insight into the issues associated with cross-cultural communication in school-family relationships, and you will learn ways to design a comprehensive communication and involvement plan in which families are partners with you in the learning of their children.

Cross-Cultural Communication: Concepts and Processes

Effective communication is an enabler of cross-cultural understanding but what are the issues and opportunities associated with communicating with students and families from non-dominant cultures? Today the peoples of the world have closer contact than ever before through computers and other electronic methods; yet the psychological distance is perhaps greater than ever. The recognition that differences have a tendency to become magnified with increased close contact, calls for concentrated effort to understand people whose beliefs and backgrounds are different from the dominant American culture. This is especially true for classroom teachers who are increasingly called upon to work with students whose family backgrounds may represent cultures from all over the world. Problems with relationships often arise when members of a cultural group look, think, talk, and act in ways that differ from the American way and they often arise out of lack of knowledge about the other culture and the ways in which culture influences how students come to know and perceive information.

Students learn the cultural patterns in which they are raised and they come to school with these patterns. Some cultures, for example, believe that a child should be seen and not heard, a belief that can operate to a student's disadvantage in American classrooms. Students learn at an early age how to speak, when it is appropriate to speak, what to speak about, and with whom to speak by following the dictates of their culture. Dissimilar communication patterns occur when interacting with someone from a different culture; consequently, familiarity with the other culture makes communication easier and more effective. The more you become involved and maintain positive relationships with families individually and collectively, the greater the opportunity for you to understand the students you serve, and for the families to feel secure in their relations with you. Communication obviously has a lot to do with developing and maintaining positive teacher-family relationships.

The Communication Process

Communication encompasses more than imparting information; it extends to the effect the message has on the receiver. Beginning most broadly with communication in general, the speaker sends the message. The nature and content of the message is affected by the speaker's knowledge and skill, and by the speaker's attitude toward himself, the listener, and subject. When sending a message, the speaker plans what to say by translating intentions into a message to send to the listener, a process called ***encoding***.

Then the speaker selects the words (verbal symbols) and the gestures (nonverbal symbols) to deliver the message. On the receiving end of this exchange is the listener, who receives the message through the senses, a process called ***decoding***. This is conditioned by the listener's knowledge of the subject and skill as a listener, and by her attitude toward herself, the speaker, and the subject. The decoding process proceeds accordingly: The message is heard, interpreted, and then evaluated to ascertain the meaning of the message and whether she agrees or disagrees with the speaker. Finally, the listener prepares a response, which may be either covert or overt.

The response, referred to as feedback, may be either verbal or nonverbal and take the overt form of, "uhu," "ok," or the covert form of smiles, nods, and frowns. The feedback may cause the speaker to adjust the message or to stop and let the listener do the speaking. As the message moves back and forth from speaker to listener and back to speaker, a factor called ***noise*** may interfere to disrupt the intended message or feedback being communicated. In cross-cultural communication, problems in understanding the language, unfamiliar nonverbal codes, and other culturally-related problems which interfere with the interpretation of what is being communicated are considered to be noise. Communication is a complicated process because so many variables come into play involving what a person says, how it is said, and how it is received. To be effective, the senders of communication need to consider the meaning of their messages and *the effect of their messages on others*. If the message is misinterpreted there is miscommunication. In working with families, particularly families from culturally-diverse groups, it is essential that your messages are sent and received as intended.

The Cross-Cultural Communication Process

Cross-cultural, or ***intercultural communication***, comes into play when and where persons from different cultures come into contact, as when a person from one culture talks to a person from another culture. Consider the speaker-listener scenario, presented earlier, with the variable of culture included. In this case, the speaker encodes a message for the listener based on his cultural background. The listener receives the message and decodes it in keeping with her cultural background. The message is transformed as it is decoded. The speaker's intended message is altered on the basis of the listener's cultural knowledge, to reflect what she thinks it means. The extent to which culture influences a cross-cultural transaction is dependent upon the similarity or dissimilarity of the cultures. The more cultures differ, the more influence culture has, and the more cultures are alike, the less influence culture has. (Klopf, 1991)

Listening, the Heart of Effective Communication

The heart of effective communication is listening for it can reduce tension and encourage trust. Listening is the most used of the communicative arts. Forty five percent of communication is spent listening; thirty percent speaking; sixteen percent reading; and nine percent writing (Klopf, 1991). Careful listening is particularly significant when communicating with families from non-dominant cultures who are more conversant in languages other than English. Through attentive listening, these family members can be more at ease and miscommunication can be detected and clarified. Moreover, since communication is a reciprocal process, family members also need to build their communication skill if they are to be effective in communicating with their child's teachers. Listening for both family members and teachers is more than hearing sounds; it is the active process of interpreting, understanding, and evaluating spoken and nonverbal speech for its message. When students' family members and teachers listen to each other, they not only increase their knowledge and understanding, they also convey an attitude of caring.

You and your family members communicate effectively when you:

- Become allies early in the relationship.
- View each other as a source of support for the child and for each other.
- Are positive, calm, quiet, and enthusiastic in your overall manner.
- Give your total attention to the person who is speaking.
- Show respect for the other person, considering his or her concerns and opinions as significant to mutual understanding.
- Keep the focus on the child and concentrate on one issue at a time.
- Listen carefully to the other person to hear what is said and what is unsaid.
- Maintain good eye contact.
- Encourage the person who is speaking by using supportive facial expressions and body language.
- Respond to the person who is speaking with attentive body language.
- Rephrase the substance and meaning of the messages you receive from the other person and try to discern the other person's meaning and feeling.
- Emphasize good points before bringing up concerns.
- Recognize that each person has unique challenges. Show empathy and an attitude of helpfulness and support to each other.
- Avoid making accusations or placing blame. Emphasize that you and students' family members are working together to help the student.
- Make use of an interpreter or mediator to assist with translations.

Special Points for Communicating with Families

Each student brings his or her family into the classroom setting and among the families there may be multiple cultures, diversity of opinion, differences in life style, and various philosophies and perceptions about working with children. In fact, it could be said that you will have only a partial view of the student until you meet and get to know the student's family. As an accompaniment to the previously outlined strategies, there are some general principles that apply when communicating and interacting with families. First and foremost, is that building positive relationships with families is an ongoing, cumulative, and personalized endeavor that happens one family at a time.

In contacts with families, you should keep the following principles in mind:

- Remember that, in addition to being a teacher of children, you are also a teacher of the families who interact with their children on a daily basis. Therefore, any classroom related topic or skill that you want families to know about and be able to do with their children, you have an obligation to teach or assure that the family member receives the necessary information or training to do so.
- Make every effort to bring out the best in family members. Support them just as you would their children and try to develop their potential.
- Avoid viewing yourself as an authority figure. Respect the family's knowledge of their children. Promote the idea of learning from each other.
- Approach the student's family at every meeting with the goal of wanting the best environment possible for their child to learn and grow.
- Avoid defensive responses and confrontations with family members. Model working together as partners.
- Convey empathy and interest in addressing family concerns. Be available, thoughtful and unhurried in your interactions with family members.
- Refrain from judging students' families just as you hope they would not make judgments about you.

Finally, remember that there are no typical families or neat categories, such as "single parent family" within which to categorize them. Each family is unique. Your openness to different lifestyles and perspectives will also enable you to learn and grow.

Building Home-School Connections

Because of their public service function, schools have more contact with families than any other agency. Families are diverse in terms of their relationships with schools, however. If their school contacts have been pleasant and successful, families are likely to enjoy visiting the school; if, their contacts have been disappointing, they will be reluctant to approach the school. Teachers are also diverse in their relationships with families. Some teachers regard working with families as a difficult and undesirable aspect of teaching. They see it as time consuming, as hard work, and even as intimidating. But, while family involvement and family education can be areas of challenge for some teachers, other teachers have found that these areas can be assets if they use a variety of techniques to communicate and are able to help families gain the skills and knowledge to help their children succeed in school.

According to families, teachers should give attention to the following areas:

- Provide a range of one on one contacts between teachers and families,
- Focus on joint problem solving between the teacher and family,
- Give precise suggestions on how families can help their children,
- Make it possible for families to attend classroom functions,
- Guide families in helping their children with homework,
- Include family members as volunteers in the classroom,
- Involve families in school governance, advocacy, and decision making,
- Draw on the resources in the community to give children and families the support they need.

It is therefore incumbent on both you and your families to communicate effectively with each other and forge the quality of human relationships that will promote cross-cultural understanding, and be mutually beneficial to the young people for whom you both have a vested interest.

Making Schools More Like Homes and Homes More Like Schools

Students and their families are linked in the education process throughout life. When education is distinguished from schooling, parents and guardians are quite naturally their children's primary educators and, through care and support, they can make a substantial difference in their son or daughter's quality of life. Because both families and educators are in a pivotal position to determine what takes place during the early years of a young person's life, the two roles should be analyzed and clarified so that they are mutually supportive. One of the opportunities for both families and educators in working with the young is to try to arrange for consistency in the school and home environments so that the child will see similarity and feel comfortable in each environment. This implies that teachers and families could seize this opportunity to work together to make schools more like homes and homes more like schools for they each have roles to play to make this possible. The big question for us in this series is how can this be done particularly in classroom settings which serve multiple cultures?

What makes a "good home" is firmly established in the minds of most teachers. Keeping in mind that schools are centered on the dominant culture, school officials are inclined to define "good homes" as those which meet the criteria of the dominant culture. A well-established belief of school officials is that families of students who are successful in school have special arrangements in their homes to encourage their children to develop organizational skills and study habits. These families, for example, have rooms set up with student desks, shelves with books, magazines, computers, and other school paraphernalia and they also have established schedules, special times, and procedures for school type activities. Beside these well-established qualities, the question is whether there are other qualities that make up a "good home?"

At the other end of the spectrum is what makes a good classroom. In recent years, many schools have made the effort to create classrooms with a more "homey" atmosphere. The classroom environments, which try to create a home-like environment, have been labeled "brain-based" because of their perceived tendencies to be intellectually stimulating. Teachers of these classrooms use table lamps to provide softer lighting, play classical-type background music, furnish the classroom with tables, cushions, and chairs instead of desks, and serve periodic snacks throughout the day that are typical of a home setting. They have also begun to employ instructional arrangements and schedules that would be more like those in less formal home-like settings. As compared to the typical traditional classroom, these efforts are commendable. However, it is interesting to ponder whether there are other models or enhancements that could be learned from those who serve non-dominant culture students?

You may have to take the lead in finding out what it is that is also effective in students' home and school environments that don't fit the dominant-culture mold. At the same time, you can seek to broaden your own horizons and those of other school officials about these qualities. Multicultural families can be included in defining and making suggestions for pedagogically effective homes and classrooms. In addition, issues related to diverse families' attempts to operate within a dominant culture institution can also be a significant part of your commitment to enhance relations with families.

The Classroom and Home as a Continuum of Learning

A report from the U. S. Department of Education (1986) emphasized a variety of ways in which you can teach families to carry the curriculum of the classroom into the home. What families do in their daily conversations, household routines, the attention they give to the student's daily work, and the concern they have for the student's progress overall, is sure to have a major impact on the student's success.

Some ways that you can offer to families to develop student's general knowledge would be by:

- Reading, talking, and listening to them.
- Telling them stories, playing games with them, and sharing hobbies.
- Discussing the news and TV programs with them.
- Providing books, supplies, and a special place for studying.
- Having a schedule and routine for meals, homework, and bedtime.

- Monitoring the content and amount of time spent watching TV, computer involvement, etc.
- Assigning and monitoring the amount of time spent in after-school jobs.
- Discussing school events.
- Helping students meet deadlines.
- Talking with students about school problems and successes.

Some simple strategies which you can offer to parents for helping the young child become a better reader from "Reading Tips for Parents" (U.S. Dept of Education, 2002) include:

- Inviting the child to read with you every day.
- Pointing word by word as you read to help the child recognize words and see that reading goes from left to right.
- Reading the child's favorite book over and over.
- Reading many stories with repeated lines and rhyming words and having the child join in on these parts.
- Discussing new words. Stopping and asking about the words. For example, this word says, 'forest.' Who do you think lives in a forest?"
- Stopping and asking about the pictures, and about what is happening in the story.
- Reading from a variety of children's books, particularly those which help them become familiar with other cultures.

Information on these government publications can be obtained by calling 1-800-USA-LEARN.

A Range of Home-School Communication Techniques

Whatever you value and hope to achieve requires a plan. This is certainly true of your communication with families. Clearly the predominance of the literature focuses on dominant culture homes, schools, and classrooms, but if you are serious about your role in creating partnerships with families in support of the education of their sons and daughters, you will think through the process and develop a plan to achieve your goals. A comprehensive communication plan for your classroom should include a variety of approaches: written, oral, face-to-face, electronic, and more general and ongoing approaches such as newsletters or student work samples. A variety of possibilities for you to consider in a comprehensive communication plan are included in this section.

Two-Way Communication

You are advised to set up a forum and procedures to maintain two-way, one on one contact with families to address some of the areas which you and your families have joint responsibility. Some ways that this can be done is through direct instruction, telephone calls, conferences, participation in classroom events, and home visits. You should consider the following approaches as you plan for ways to promote ***two-way communication*** in which you are able to send a message and at the same time receive a response/ feedback.

A Special Class for Parents

Dealing with the complexities of being an effective parent or guardian, requires considerable skill irrespective of culture. Yet, parenting is generally taken for granted by the population-at-large. There is very little formal training, assistance, or opportunity for families to move beyond their intuitive parenting styles and strategies to explore some of the issues and possibilities that are inherent in child rearing. School officials, for instance, make the assumption that parents and guardians are to cooperate and help their children learn, but few specifics are given as to how this can be done. It is reasonable to presume, though, that if parents and guardians are to be partners in their children's learning, they need to know how to assist in the learning process. This, of course, means knowing as much as possible about what is taught in school, so that families can determine the ways in which they can help. In keeping with the premise of this professional development series that teachers are responsible for teaching everything they want students to know, they would therefore be expected to teach and support families in learning how to be an effective partner in their child's education. Families should know the most promising educational practices and how to use them at home to help their children.

A class, which you or the school-as-a-whole could set up for your families, is one way for you to speak directly to families of all cultures and assist them in a variety of areas that you deem important to a successful schooling experience. The classes would also provide an opportunity for you hear the views of families, non-dominant culture families in particular, on the topics and issues. In the class, you and your families have an opportunity to discuss the essential qualities of education, the role of school and home, and other topics of special interest to families.

Some of the topics which could be covered in such a class for families include:

- The Nature of the School-Family Partnership
- The School's Learning Expectations for Student Achievement
- The Home Environment, Homework, Books, and Other Resources
- The Performance Exhibition, What It Means for You and Your Child
- Volunteering Your Talents in the Classroom
- Issues and Topics of Special Interest to Families

In the introductory meeting with families, the discussion could be devoted to exploring *what it means to be a partner with the teacher and child in an enduring educational venture.* Undoubtedly, a topic such as this would have greater impact if it were held on a school-wide basis since most families have children in more than one class and can obtain a broader perspective on the school program. And certainly, the agenda for some of the class meetings could be tailored to the unique needs and interests of the participants. However, topics such as the learning expectations and activities from grade to grade throughout the school and the ways in which students are called upon to demonstrate their learning would certainly be of interest to most families. Topics such as the importance of talking and reading to children, ways to help with homework, and how to make use of the community's resources for learning would also be very likely to attract many families.

Many long-term benefits can accrue from these special classes. Families who participate in the classes, are able not only to increase their own knowledge, but are also able to provide support and advice to others in the community. This can lead to fostering the goals of caring and cross-cultural understanding beyond the school and classroom to the school community at large. When you offer your special talents to the families of your students, the rewards are sure to come.

An Open-Door Policy

Although a series of activities such as open houses, meetings, forums and seminars can contribute to a receptive climate in the classroom, your open-door policy would clearly be the ultimate in achieving and maintaining positive teacher-family relationships. An open-door policy can best be described as an attitude which conveys that parents are welcome at any time in your classroom. It would suggest that the classroom is the child's home and that families are very important participants and contributors to what goes on in their children's home away from home. It avoids the "problem conference" syndrome by encouraging dialogue between teachers and families before a problem develops. It allows you to establish two-way communication in an open forum and set the stage for families and you to work together on behalf of the student.

Early Communication

When you make early contacts with families, you are being proactive. These positive early interchanges with families can help you feel comfortable in your involvement with families. You will find that early communication with the families of your class, even during the summer before school starts, can be well worth the time and effort. You can send letters to welcome each new student to your class. Or, if you are a teacher of young children, you can even have an orientation session with families prior to the opening of school to ease the student into the classroom setting. Orientation sessions can be used at other grade levels with equal success and gratification. What a way to welcome families who are new to the school or new to American culture! These early contacts demonstrate that you care. They establish rapport before school begins, and they promote an immediate open-door attitude.

Telephone Calls

A telephone call early in the school year followed by periodic calls to families to establish relationships produces many benefits. Positive telephone calls can be made to obtain parents commitment to attend school or classroom meetings. This would be particularly important for an essential early meeting like the Back-to-School Orientation. When making these early calls, however, you should be prepared to hear families ask, "What's wrong," since most often telephone calls from the teacher immediately signal that something is amiss. A note from you to set up the telephone meeting can be helpful.

Home Visits

Home visits may be the only way to reach some parents or guardians and these visits can be a rewarding experience for you and your families. However, you need to let the family know you are coming, the purpose of the visit, and request a time or option of meeting at another place since not all families are receptive to home visits. It is also acknowledged that many teachers are skeptical of making home visits as well. If you decide to make home visits, you should recognize that some families are afraid that you may have ulterior motives for making a visit to their home and, as a result, you should take all precautions to make families feel at ease. Once home visits become accepted practice and are less threatening, both you and your families are likely to look forward to them.

Special Recognitions—Families of the Week

A special note can be written by the student to invite a member of his or her family to visit the classroom as the family of the week. As part of the visit, members of the family can attend to give information about the family. Pictures of the family and student can be posted on the bulletin board, for example, and the student can bring in information and important facts, stories, customs, and other things about the family that make it unique. Special weekly recognition of families should include all families rather than families of specific cultures even though, these recognitions can be useful in culturally diverse classrooms. Many teachers depend on families to serve as ambassadors of their respective cultures and to inform the class about their culture. Remember, though, it is not the families' responsibility to teach about cultures. They may be called upon to augment what you do, but as in other areas of the curriculum, you must provide the leadership in teaching what students should know.

Conferences

Conferences between you and designated family members promote cooperation between you and your families. They are of the greatest benefit because they provide a forum for ongoing communication between you and your families throughout the year. Conferences are avenues for personal two-way communication between you and a family member or three-way communication between you, the student, and a family member. All parties involved, recognize the conference as the most conducive forum for developing a supportive team to work in behalf of the student. Conferences between you and a student's family member have come to be viewed by families and teachers alike as being so valuable that most schools release students from classes to schedule conferences two or three times a year. These school-based conferences, however, should not take the place of you setting up personal conferences as needed with individual students and their families. Because of the organizational commitment by the school system to set up one or more regular or mandatory conferences, it should be more convenient for you and your families to arrange additional conferences as needed.

. You can plan for a well-organized conference by sending a reminder and brief points that will be covered in the conference. Your attentive behavior and body language, warm tone of voice and clear articulation during the conference will communicate a positive message. You should refrain from projecting an aura of "we against them" in support of the school and its practices, for if you adopt this posture, you can cause family members to be defensive. On the other hand, if you are sensitive to their role and needs, you will convey an attitude of advocacy toward families. You will give each family member your time and full attention, you will be honest and open and refrain from acting superior, you will recognize that everyone wants the best for their child, and, you will give families a prominent role in the education of their children.

The recommendations for two-way communication in conferences are also applicable to other forms of two-way communication. The points are valuable for you and your families to know and develop as part of an ongoing working relationship. You can establish rapport with families by building your communication skills, by making special efforts to communicate with families from cultures other than the dominant mainstream culture, and by using interpreters to communicate with families whose first language is not English

One-Way Communication

There are times when you send messages in the form of ***one-way communication***. This form of communication does not provide immediate feedback but is often needed to inform families about the school's plans and events. Typical vehicles for one-way communication include newsletters, notes and letters, newspapers, handbooks, and media announcements and presentations.

Newsletters

A *newsletter* is designed to be an ongoing form of one way communication which you should send home on a regular basis to communicate classroom events ranging from curriculum activities, field trips, contributions of families and others, and accomplishments by individual students. Some other suggestions for newsletters include a calendar of classroom events, book suggestions, birthday recognitions, and children's quotes. In essence, newsletters can be a source for educating and motivating families to support and become involved in classroom events and activities. Your newsletters should be carefully designed with attractive visuals and graphic layout, the message should be thoughtful and careful attention should be given to grammar, correct spelling, etc. To be effective as a source of school-family communication, the schedule for distributing the newsletter should adhered to *faithfully*. A monthly distribution schedule, on the first day of the month, generally works well. Preparing for the distribution of weekly newsletters can be demanding; however, with desk top publishing programs the preparation of well-designed weekly newsletters can be more feasible now than in the past.

Student Work Samples

One of the best ways to keep families informed and involved in the educational program and work of their children is to send home current papers depicting students' actual work, **student work samples,** on a regular basis, at least once weekly along with a note or statement from you about the work. Students are eager to share their weekly work and families look forward to this method of staying informed about their son or daughter's progress. There's nothing like seeing the actual assignments and visible evidence of their child's performance. Assignments should be meaningful and of high quality, for parents will be noting your skill in making assignments as much as they will be attending to their child's performance on the assignment. Assure that the type of work that you are assigning is not likely to be viewed by families as busy work.

Newspapers and Yearbooks

Families are most interested in newspapers and yearbooks when they contain articles and photographs that involve their children. Consequently, you should take care to assure that these communication devices give a broad representation of students. Newspapers and yearbooks are significant in their own way and may provide useful leadership opportunities for students, particularly at the secondary level. As a source of direct communication between schools and homes, however, other forms of written communication are more appropriate.

Handbooks

Handbooks are usually developed for use at the school or district level, but there are occasions when a special handbook related to a grade level, academic program, or classroom can supplement to the school handbook and be an effective source of information for families. For example, as an individual classroom practitioner, you may choose to clarify your classroom rules and procedures and other classroom policies in the form of a mini handbook.

Media Sources and Presentations

Usually school districts designate an official to work with the mass media to get publicity and present newsworthy articles to newspapers, radio, and television sources. You can be influential, however, in alerting your principal and other officials about newsworthy events taking place in your classroom that you want to publicize. Also, with the use of computer technology, you and your students may develop power point presentations on special topics for presentation to families or others. School programs and events that are centered on the actual work and performance of students are found to be the most meaningful to families and students and, to the extent that they can be publicized, even greater support can be achieved. Such programs can set the stage for learning and they are excellent avenues for including families in the process.

Email Messages, Notes and Letters

With the age of computer technology individual notes often in the form of email have become more commonplace than in the past. Email messages can be used for specific correspondence between you and your families because they allow for interactive conversation. Families who have access to a computer appreciate these email messages and, of course, they continue to appreciate special handwritten notes with the teacher's personal touch as well. Notes and letters may be used for various purposes as in the case of introductory letters sent prior to the beginning of school or as an extension to your newsletter to provide reminders, suggestions, etc. Their most frequent use in classrooms today is as a source of motivation to inform family members when a student is doing well. The idea is to communicate in a positive manner at just the right time to build a supportive relationship with the family and enhance the student's self-concept. The key to an effective "good news" note is its timeliness, spontaneity, and sincerity.

Family Participation in Classroom Learning Events

Back to School Orientation

This school and classroom event for the families of a school where I served as principal began informally. Prompted by my personal experience with the extensive orientation process of some private schools, it became for me a teaching opportunity for our faculty to set the stage for our work with students and their families in the coming school year. It continued as other schools became interested and also wanted to introduce families to their educational program and give them a meaningful role in the learning of their sons and daughters. These early efforts by a small group of teachers and administrators have now evolved to become a time-tested event for many schools and classrooms. They allow teachers *from preschool through high school* to spend one afternoon or evening each year actually teaching families about the experiences their sons and daughters will have with them over the course of the school year. You will want to be among these teachers.

On this Back-to-School occasion, families have an opportunity to put themselves in the place of their son or daughter as they are taught specific ways in which they can be involved in working with students to assure success over the course of the year. The agenda for the session can include the subjects and topics to be covered at a particular grade level, classroom management procedures and expectations, assessment and grading policies, special events and dates, and communication plans. Back-to-School orientation sessions may be held at various times during the day, evenings, or on weekends to accommodate parents but should be held as early as possible during the school year. It is not a time for students or for discussing individual students, however. Events involving students can occur later in the school year, at Open House for example. Here the audience includes adult family members learning from the teacher how they can work together in behalf of their sons and daughters.

Open House

The traditional Open House event has endured over the years and continues to be a significant part of school life for families, students, and teachers. During Open House classrooms are on display and often students serve as hosts and hostesses to their families in welcoming them, introducing them to their teachers, and explaining classroom activities. Open House usually occurs during the fall, where applicable, shortly after Back-to-School Night and focuses on showcasing the classrooms and student work.

The Performance Exhibition

The Performance Exhibition, presented first in *Module One* as the major focus of student assessment, is designed to be the highlight of the school year. In this event students demonstrate their learning in various areas of the curriculum with family members and community members as the audience. The exhibition occurs at the end of the year and is the result of you, your students, and their families working together to assist students in developing, refining, and exhibiting their learning. The Performance Exhibition plays a prominent role in the education program and in achieving the objectives of this professional development series.

The Performance Exhibition sets up a goal-oriented process which promotes a culturally-centered learning community where classroom practice throughout the school year is focused on cooperation among students and families from multiple cultures in the interest of student learning. Through this overarching focus on families assisting their children in achieving significant learning outcomes, family involvement that has often been a contrived and dubious activity in classrooms, becomes credible and real. Students have the opportunity to capitalize on their multiple talents and unique styles to learn and to demonstrate their learning in multiple authentic ways. The curriculum through this process is implemented in ways that can move students and families beyond the usual mainstream American method such that the goal of building cross-cultural understanding is a natural result. In the process of working together, students and their families have the opportunity to add to their background knowledge about their own culture, to help others learn about their culture, and also to learn about the cultures of others.

Working with Families as Volunteers

You can call upon the families of your students to serve the classroom in a variety of ways. Families can share their talents with students, they can serve as volunteers to assist you in a variety of classroom initiatives, and they can serve as tutors to their own children at home and as classroom assistants to all children in the classroom. They can help with all-school projects such as publishing books for students, and they can lend support and address the issue of school holidays by planning and serving as hosts and hostesses in selected all school and classroom events. Each of these areas, however, requires planning and some require training to enable family and community members to carry out the tasks. Whenever family or community members are called upon to participate in classrooms, whether as tutors or other classroom assistants, *you need to provide the teaching, training, and guidance, whatever is necessary* to assure the success of the family member in the volunteering role.

Volunteers to Share Their Talents

Family members from other cultures can share many things with students about their culture including history, geography, lifestyle, and traditions. Some family members may have musical, artistic, or other talents and could be called upon to give culturally enhancing presentations for the students. Folk singing, playing drums, or other indigenous instruments from a family member's country of origin, for example, would be a very special asset. Some families may have hobbies such as basket making or quilting that could support cross-cultural understanding as an area of interest in the classroom. Family members, community members, and celebrities enjoy having the opportunity to come to class to read a book that they enjoy to the students. If these volunteers have books or stories about their culture, they could be a valuable resource for the students as the class seeks to increase its cross-cultural understanding.

Volunteers to Assist with Class Projects

A family involvement project that has become very popular for classrooms and family members is ***book publishing***. The project calls for students to develop a narrative or non-fiction piece of writing on a given topic or theme during a class session and, after the text is complete, have it bound by a cadre of family and community members who have received training in the book publishing process. Schools may purchase book binding and laminating equipment and set aside a work area for family and community volunteers to publish the books. There are a variety of methods for preparing the text (handwritten or typed), and a variety of materials and methods for binding from hand sewing to stapling. Book publishing can be a creative project for the students, teachers, and family-community volunteers to work together to plan the content, form, and presentation of the books. Depending on the commitment of everyone involved, the process and product can have great potential and be far reaching.

Volunteers to Serve as Classroom Tutors

Tutoring gives the needed help to students which many family members are very much interested in providing. It should be remembered, however, that *tutoring requires skill and, consequently, if you wish to have family and community members assist your students in this way, you must be sure that those who volunteer to tutor students are carefully trained to do so.* Workshops or training sessions can be arranged to provide family members with strategies for helping students with various subjects in the classroom and to teach individual family members various ways to assist students at home. Tutoring can be extended to summer vacation through teacher encouragement and the willingness of students and families to participate. Summer can be an opportune time for student remediation; however, activities during the summer should be an alternative to the course of study during the school year. Activities which strengthen students' thinking skills in a natural setting, for example, such as planning the meals and developing the budget for a week, can be used to develop students' knowledge of nutrition, budget, etc. as an alternative to the traditional way of teaching math.

Volunteers to Host Special Days and Events

Family members as volunteers can be encouraged to participate in school events, activities, and academic exercises. With respect to holidays, families can use their influence and involvement in the community and work with the school to identify, organize, and help to host special holiday celebrations and events. Considering the history and context surrounding some of the holidays traditionally celebrated in the schools, however, you should take the lead in setting the parameters for this activity. Volume I of this series offers some insights on classroom holiday celebrations and families from non-dominant cultures can also provide their unique perspective on holiday celebrations. Essentially, care should be taken to consider the perspectives of all students and the impact of the event on enhancing or detracting from cross-cultural understanding and excellence in learning. This professional development series calls for fewer traditional holiday celebrations in schools and classrooms and more events to present and celebrate students' learning in the culturally-centered education program.

A winter event, a spring time event, and a student recognition and last-day-of-school ceremony and picnic are the recommended possibilities. Such events would more likely be viewed as neutral, more in line with the role and mission of the school, and supported by families of all cultures. These events would have an academic focus and would call for the full involvement of all families in supporting the event, contributing food and socialization opportunities. Family members can look upon these occasions as their opportunities to do something special such as provide refreshments and other tokens to help students feel extra-special. In response, students can do something special for families in the form of thank you letters, hand-made gifts, and special programs such as a Family Day.

The Performance Exhibition: A Ten-Step Process for Involving Families and their Children in Learning

Thinking back on the two modules of this volume, you now have the opportunity to review and consider how the culturally-centered education program and activities in this school-community initiative can be implemented in your classroom and school. This section of the module should be coordinated with *Module One* which explains the education program and the student assessment strategies that are applied in this exhibition of learning.

The process, referred to here as ***beginning with the end in mind***, has made it possible for us to reach our destination. It called for thinking long term over the entire school year planning, teaching, and assessing what students needed to know and be able to do at the end of the school year. Throughout the year you, your students, and your families worked diligently to prepare students to demonstrate their learning in the seven recommended curriculum strands through their portfolios, projects, and performances. Now we are ready for THE SHOW, THE "BIG GAME, THE RECITAL, ***THE PERFORMANCE EXHIBITION.***

Let's take stock and reflect on what we did to get here? The curriculum strands and performance instruments and the communication and family involvement strategies have been explained in previous sections of this volume. This section addresses their use and sequence in preparing for the End of Year Performance Exhibition. This is a review with some directions for ways that you can implement the coordinated sequence of the Ten Events which lead to the Performance Exhibition.

1. Set the Stage for the Process in an Introductory Letter.

The sequence begins with the ***introductory letter*** from you to each family. This letter provides a friendly introduction—who you are, a bit about your background, and your goals for their son or daughter. It also explains the performance exhibition in a general way, what you hope to accomplish during the year, and ways that families can be involved in their child's education. It tells them that you are eager to meet them and that you look forward to seeing them at the Back-to-School Orientation, where they will receive a full explanation of the education program, the performance exhibition, and special ways that they can be involved in the learning of their son or daughter. Keep the letter simple, brief, warm, and to the point. Try to put it in the mail at least a week before the opening of school.

2. Initiate the Program and Process at Back-to-School Orientation.

This is the one big opportunity that you will have to provide information and instruction to family members about the culturally-centered education program, including the performance exhibition, and your expectations for their son or daughter. It is the time, specifically set aside for you to teach your students' family members and gain their support. Your enthusiasm is therefore crucial to the success of the meeting.

The end-of year Performance Exhibition provides the target for what you expect students to accomplish and be able to demonstrate at the end of the year. This early informational meeting provides the forum for you to convey the significance of this end-of-year celebration of learning and to tell all family members that their presence, and enthusiastic support to you and to students along the way, will assure successful student performances.

The preparation and professionalism that you convey to families through your explanation of the classroom procedures and expectations during this Back to School event will encourage an initial positive impression of you and of the education their son or daughter is receiving. Even more, your explanation of the curriculum performance expectations and their assessment through portfolios, projects, and performances will provide even greater assurance of your competence in providing a high quality educational experience for their sons and daughters. Finally, an explanation of ways that families can work with their son or daughter at home to prepare for in the concluding performance at the end of the year lets families know that they too have a role to play and a stake in the outcomes of their child's learning. Your explanation of their role should begin at this meeting.

Time should be provided for questions and explanations of the meetings and activities to follow this meeting. The participants at this meeting should leave knowing that this meeting is an orientation to other sessions that will occur throughout the year. An agenda and folder containing samples of the topics covered in the session, which parents will need for future reference, should be provided to each family such as:

1. The grade level curriculum and performance expectations
2. The classroom management procedures, behavioral expectations and consequences
3. A description and process for students to develop their portfolios, projects, and performances, and how this will be coordinated over the course of the year and evaluated at the end of the year.
4. The sequence of events and meetings leading to the performance exhibition
5. Suggestions for family involvement
6. Sign-up sheets with categories for families to volunteer and assist

3. Chart the Course in Goal Setting Conferences.

As soon as possible after the Back-to-School Orientation, begin to set up three-way conferences (student, family member(s), and teacher) to discuss personally with each family the information that was shared in the Back-to-School Orientation meeting. This early conference allows you to get to know the family members on a personal basis, to learn about their backgrounds, interests, and expectations of you. It is also the time to gain each family's commitment to work with their child throughout the school year. Similarly, it is also the time for the families to give input to you regarding what they would like to have happen in the classroom, what their individual needs are, and the special contributions they would be willing to give to the classroom effort. The conference is likely to be most beneficial if the child and even other members of the family attend this conference to make the entire family an important part of the team.

4. Use Newsletters to Motivate and Keep Families on Track.

Plan your sequence of newsletters so that parents have a time frame for expecting these formal, ongoing means of communication from you. Once per month on the first of the month is recommended. Other scheduled times may work well also as long as they are consistent and in keeping with the performance exhibition sequence. The newsletter needs to be warm but also precise and business-like. Emphasize "we" in your language. It should set up important dates and events and be a source of information and motivation. The Newsletter makes it possible for you to address on a consistent basis, how the planning, efforts and progress of the class, and successes of families toward readiness for the Performance Exhibition are proceeding.

The format can be set up in a variety of ways with the dates and events appearing first, followed by explanations, motivational appeals, and always something from the students. Some teachers have also found a calendar format to be useful. Computer word processing is very helpful to producing a professional document that can reveal so much about you as a teacher. Do your best to create an informative polished document. It will be well-worth the effort in terms of benefits to you and your families.

5. Send Illustrative Student Work Samples Home Weekly.

A high priority for Families is the opportunity to see the actual work that their child is doing in the classroom on a regular basis. This is the opportunity for you to convey the progress that the student is making on day-to-day assignments. It is very important for you to set up arrangements to send work samples home at least once weekly with an explanation of the nature of the assignment and brief comments to give insights on the student's effort and achievement with respect to the assignment. Many teachers prefer to send work home in a packet each Friday with a request that Family members review the papers, sign and return the packet the following Monday. This process gives an ongoing report of the student's written work. The Performance Portfolio containing samples of these day-to-day assignments will be on display at the end-of-year Performance Exhibition.

6. Set up Student-Family Projects.

The three-dimensional work of students that doesn't fit neatly into a portfolio can also be very revealing about student performance and the extent to which the student is able to engage in long-term assignments, individually or in a cooperative group effort, and carry them through to completion. Many projects may also carry a family component where family members may also participate with the student(s) in conducting an aspect of the assignment. In most instances, the projects would have a multicultural emphasis and may encourage family members to contribute appropriately.

7. Display Student Work at Open House.

Open Houses in schools have usually served as the first opportunity for Families to come to school to meet the teachers and see the classrooms. They have traditionally been a time of excitement for students and their families to see firsthand who the teacher is and where the child spends the entire day every day. In the past, however, little information has been provided to families about the substance of the educational program for the school year at this or any other event. Most teachers can recall the typical Open House event with its open-ended format.

The challenge in working toward the Performance Exhibition is to harness the enthusiasm with which students and families approach Open House and focus it on the goals of the performance exhibition. Since students and families will be fully involved in the program of learning, Open House can be an opportune time to display the early phases of students work products—portfolios, projects, in particular. Seeing the possibilities for what can be accomplished can be very motivating to all students and families in ways that would secure their involvement more readily in the learning of their children. The display of projects in various stages of completion makes the point that the process is equal in importance to the finished product. Completed projects will be displayed and explained as part of the end of year Performance Exhibitions.

8. Communicate Progress toward Exhibitions on Conference Day.

About the time of the usual first conference, teachers, students, and their family members would be ready to sit down and assess their progress and readiness for the Performance Exhibition. What are the areas of strength and what areas need more attention. Teachers speak about the progress they see in classroom performance and family members speak about ways that they are assisting and supporting the learning goals at home. Each person is involved and has this focus, something to contribute to assessing the status of their efforts to meet the learning goals.

9. Conduct Monthly Interim Performance Exhibitions.

Hold practice performances throughout the year within the class or with other classes serving as the audience. The objective is to have groups of students demonstrate their progress in various areas of the curriculum for practice in front of others. For example, students may read a selection that they have practiced for fluency, they may explain the strategies they used to solve a math problem, or they may be asked to name and explain the climate and lifestyles of people in certain regions across the globe. Family members, of course, may be encouraged to attend these sessions and to set up similar practice sessions at home. The more opportunities that students have to practice, the more skilled and confident they will become.

10. Put it All Together in End-of-Year Performance Exhibitions.

The opportunity to perform before others can be an intimidating experience, but after a year of preparation the students will be ready. Families and the entire community will be there as a base of support. A full explanation of the Performance Exhibition, its purpose, connection to the grade level curriculum, and portion of the assessment to be displayed before a public audience is provided in *Module One*. Essentially, however, students as groups and individuals have the opportunity to display their talents and strengths through their portfolios, projects, and performances in areas that they have worked to develop over the course of the school year.

Even though the performance is the highlight, the involvement leading to the performance is equal in significance. The process of interacting and working together with others from a variety of cultures, backgrounds, and perspectives toward a common effort is a meaningful undertaking for you, your students, and your families. Family members are sure to attend because they have been involved in all aspects of preparing for this culminating event. And to have every one there for this very special occasion to celebrate together can truly be a source of pride for all.

The group diverse group of classroom teachers was asked to discuss ways that they would communicate with and actively involve parents in their child's learning. They responded accordingly:

Classroom Teachers Talk It Over

"The biggest problem that I have with parents from different cultural groups is the language barrier, especially during parent conferences. Now they usually bring a family member to help with a translation. I am going to request that the school provide a translator."

"My families are really supportive of what I do in the classroom. I teach the regular curriculum and this is what they want. They have told me that they don't want me to make adjustments for their children."

"Working with my parents is my favorite part of teaching. I take pride in what I do to communicate with them and involve them. I am always sending work home. I send letters and notes home on a regular basis and I am always making phone calls. The main thing is that I try to get to know each of my parents on a personal basis. The one thing I would add is the use of a newsletter."

"I think the greatest thing about this module is the exhibitions. I like to have my students do performances and have their parents come in to see them perform. I'm going to do this a little more now and have some of the parents help them."

"I always use portfolios to collect student work, but now I am going to do this in a more organized fashion. I think the idea of using them for parent conferences is great! I appreciate getting so many wonderful ideas from this module."

As you conclude this module, consider the views of these classroom teachers and be prepared to give your view? How do your thoughts about working with families compare with the views expressed by these classroom teachers?

Summary of Module Two

This module, which concludes *Module Two* of the Culturally-Centered Education Program volume of the professional development series, is concerned with how you can enhance your work in the classroom through positive home-school relations. It completes the goal of showing how a culturally-centered educational program can build cross-cultural understanding and promote excellence in student learning. Hopefully, now, these two essential areas, a culturally-centered education program supported through partnerships with families can form the core of your classroom practice.

From this module, you should know the significance and have some important strategies to encourage effective communication and meaningful family involvement in student learning.

In review, some specific points are:

- The module has shown how supportive family relationships can enhance classroom practice and build cross-cultural understanding. Two major points were presented. One point was that structuring meaningful family communication and involvement in the learning of the classroom is enhancing. Another point was that many cultures have an orientation which values the collective family over individual child. Your recognition of different cultural orientations can build cross-cultural understanding in the context of supportive family relationships.

- In this module, you have been introduced to cross-cultural communication, the processes involved, and some effective techniques to employ. Dissimilar communication patterns can occur when interacting with another culture; therefore, familiarity with the other culture was suggested as important to effective cross-cultural communication. Listening was presented as the heart of effective communication.

- The module has stressed ways to create effective home-school connections by making the classroom and home a continuum of learning so that the student sees similarity and feels comfortable in each environment. The point was made to broaden the criteria for what makes a "good" home. Multicultural families can be involved in offering suggestions for setting up the classroom.

- A range of communication techniques, both one way and two way, with emphasis on having an open door policy were presented. Ways to employ a variety of techniques have been identified and described in the module. Communicating clearly and often with positive reports and developing a plan for working as a supportive team in behalf of students in student-teacher-family conferences were presented as productive approaches.

- Strategies for ways to work with families throughout the year have been suggested in this module. Family members can serve in very helpful and influential ways in the classroom and they are very often eager to volunteer their services. When family members volunteer to serve in classrooms, however, classroom teachers should assure that they have the necessary preparation and training to carry out the designated roles that they are asked to perform.

- In coordination with *Module One*, ways to implement The Performance Exhibition as the focal point of learning has been outlined through a ten-step process for involving families with their children in learning. The Performance Exhibition is the culmination for all of the activities leading to this end-of-year event. Ways to develop and use the portfolio, the project, and the performance as part of the built-in structures of classroom practice are explained in the module.

This module concludes the involvement of families in the culturally-centered educational program and your use of the education program as a source for enabling students to extend their perspectives beyond dominant culture information to build broader and deeper understandings of the world and its peoples.

Opening Scenario (Afterthoughts)

What do you believe are the issues surrounding the lack of motivation which students in the case have toward school? Please give examples to explain some specific insights that have been gained from the module that you would use in your classroom to motivate students, parents, and community members to want to become interested and involved in your classroom.

Questions/Activities

1. Explain the following concepts in relationship to communicating with families and involving them in your classroom:

Intercultural communication   two-way communication
Beginning with the end in mind   noise   decoding

2. Explain the communication process. What are some implications for working with families from non-dominant cultures?

3. Explain what you would do to minimize "noise" in intercultural communication in your interactions with families.

4. Explain how what goes on in classrooms can affect families positively or negatively and give either give support or lack of support to the school?

5. Describe some two-way and some one-way forms of communication that you would use in your classroom. When and why would you use these forms of communication?

6. Explain, step-by-step how you would carry out a comprehensive program of involving families in the learning of their children. Use the concept of "End of Year Performance Exhibitions" as your model.

7. Summarize the new ideas, principles, and concepts that you learned in this module and explain how you will implement these new insights in your classroom.

<u>Cooperative Group Activity:</u>

Conduct research to obtain additional information on the current lifestyles, perspectives, and issues associated with the five cultural groups that are presented in this module. Present your findings to the class in a panel discussion.

Looking in Classrooms

Visit a classroom in your area for the purpose of finding out how the teacher addresses cultural diversity in relationship to communicating and involving parents in the classroom. Observe and note the following. (Ask questions of the teacher in areas where you need clarification.)

1. Describe the ways in which the teacher communicates with parents, families, and members of the community.

2. In what ways are families involved in the schools. Are parents and family members directly involved in the learning of their children? Please explain.

Following your visitation, write a <u>Brief Summary Statement</u> to explain what you found out in this visit, describing the ways in which the teacher communicates with and involves parents in the classroom. What communication and educational approaches would you use with parents in your own classroom to enhance cross-cultural understanding.

Recommendations for Further Reading

Berger, Eugenia H. *Parents as Partners in Education: Families and Schools Working Together*. Upper Saddle River, Inc.: Pearson, Merrill, Prentice Hall, 2004.

> This book offers numerous ways to communicate with parents and numerous possibilities for helping families assist their children in learning to read and learn other subject matter.

Epstein, J. L. & M. G. Sanders. "Family, School, and Community Partnerships." In M. Bornstein (Ed.), *Handbook of Parenting* (2$^{nd\ ed}$). Mahwah, NJ.: Lawrence Erlbaum, 2002.

> Epstein's work has been very influential in the literature on family-school relationships. Here he emphasizes partnerships in ways that are discussed in this book.

Klopf, Donald W. *Intercultural Encounters: The Fundamentals of Intercultural Communication*. Englewood, Co.: Morton Publishing Co., 1991.

> This book points out the difficulty of communicating across cultures. A number of strategies are offered to assist readers in intercultural encounters.

Vang, Christopher T. "Minority Parents Should Know More about School Culture and Its Impact on Their Children's Education." *Multicultural Education*. 14, no. 3 (April 1, 2007): 32-40.

> The impact of American mainstream culture in schools and classrooms on non-mainstream students is shared with minority parents.

The MASS Professional Development Series in Review

Throughout the four-volume series the concern is to set forth principles, strategies, and practices to improve classroom practice in ways that promote excellence in student learning. Educational excellence, as emphasized in each volume of the series, is dependent upon having a broader view of schooling than the traditional western-oriented view. Consequently, the twin goals of building cross-cultural understanding and promoting excellence in student learning are closely linked in this professional development series.

The series explains why many students, particularly those whose forbears did not make the choice to be part of American culture, have been resistant to or reluctant to fully embrace what goes on in American classrooms. Even if the schools were to succeed in getting all students to embrace what the school offers, it would still be inadequate because, as explained in this and other volumes of the series, the philosophical underpinnings upon which American schools are based, fail to embrace all available knowledge. It is limited to Anglo-European culture and functions to induct all students into the American way of life. This has been and continues to be problematic because it has imposed limitations on what students learn and how they learn it in the context of American classrooms.

The limitations on classroom practice in American schools have been revised and extended in Volumes II-IV in which culturally-compatible practices in classroom management, the education program and the teaching process are outlined. This is the second of the three classroom practice volumes. In this volume readers learned how to counter the limitations on what students learn and how they learn it through the education program. A descriptive model and strategies for designing and implementing a culturally-centered education program were spelled out in this volume as vehicle for promoting cross-cultural understanding and excellence in student learning. A variety of methods to communicate with families and involve them in their child's learning were also emphasized.

Even though the cultural phenomenon is highlighted in the four volumes of the series, it surely becomes clear to readers over the course of study in the series, that culturally-compatible classroom practice is simply effective classroom practice. It benefits students from non-dominant cultures but it benefits mainstream American students even more. Moreover, application of the recommended classroom practices does not require radical change in what is already established as fundamentally sound classroom practice. The necessary change—stressed in each volume of the series—is to have teachers become "transforming intellectuals" who think about and analyze what they do, and then act in accordance with truth, accuracy, and openness in the interest of all students.

The MASS (Model Alternative School Services) *Professional Development Series for Excellence in Teaching and Learning* sets forth a coordinated approach for examining and improving classroom practice. MASS, through its publications and services is thorough and comprehensive in providing materials and assistance based in the needs of individual clients and schools. MASS consultants are prepared to help teachers develop the curriculum and put the conceptual knowledge derived from this volume of the professional development series into action in their daily classroom practice.

Contact us at www.schoolin.org

References, Vol. 1-4

Adler, Mortimer J. *The Paideia Proposal, An Educational Manifesto.* New York: Macmillan, 1982.

Anderson, James D. *The Education of Blacks in the South, 1860-1935.* Chapel Hill: University of North Carolina Press, 1988.

Anderson, L. M.., N. L Brubaker, J, Allerman-Brooks, and G. Duffy. "A Qualitative Study of Seatwork in First-Grade Classrooms." *Elementary School Journal* (1985) 86, 123-140.

Anderson, Richard C., Elfrieda H. Hiebert, Judith A. Scott, and Ian A. G. Wilkinson. *Becoming A Nation of Readers: The Report of the Commission on Reading.* Washington D.C., 1985.

Apple, M. *Official Language: Democratic Education in a Conservative Age.* New York: Routledge, 1993.

Baloche, Lynda. *The Cooperative Classroom: Empowering Learning.* Upper Saddle River, New Jersey: Prentice Hall, 1998.

Bandura, Albert. *Self Efficacy: The Exercise of Control.* New York: Freeman, 1997.

Bandura, Albert. *Social Foundations of Thought and Action: A Social Cognitive Theory.* Upper Saddle River, New Jersey: Prentice Hall, 1986.

Bandura, Albert. *Social Learning Theory.* Upper Saddle River, N.J.: Prentice Hall, 1977.

Banks, James. *An Introduction to Multicultural Education.* Boston: Allyn and Bacon, 2002.

Banks, James. "Multicultural Literacy and Curriculum Reform," *Educational Horizons,* 69 (3), 135-140.

Banks, James, McGee, and C. Banks, eds. *Multicultural Education: Issues and Perspectives*, Hoboken, NJ: Wiley, 2004.

Bennett, Christine I. *Comprehensive Multicultural Education, 6th ed.* Boston: Pearson Education, 2007.

Berger, Eugenia H. *Parents as Partners in Education: Families and Schools Working Together.* Upper Saddle River, Inc.: Pearson, Merrill, Prentice Hall, 2004.

Bergstrom, A., L. M. Cleary, and Peacock. *Seventh Generation: Native Students Speak About Finding the Good Path.* Charleston, WV: ERIC Clearinghouse on Rural Education and Small Schools, 2003.

Berlin, Ira. *Many Thousands Gone: The First Two Centuries of Slavery in North America.* Cambridge MA: Harvard University Press, 1998.

Bloom, Benjamin S. *Human Characteristics and School Learning.* New York: McGraw-Hill, 1976.

Bloom, Benjamin, ed. *Developing Talent in Young People.* New York: Ballantine Books, 1985.

Brophy, Jere. "Successful Teaching Strategies for the Inner City Child." *Phi Delta Kappa* (1982) 63, 527-530.

Brophy, Jere. "Synthesis of Research on Strategies for Motivating Students to Learn." *Educational Leadership* (1987) 45, 2, 40-48.

Brophy, Jere. and M. McCoslin. "Teachers' Reports of How They Perceive and Cope with Problem Students." *Elementary School Journal* 93, 1 (1992): 3-68.

Brown, Dee. *Bury My Heart at Wounded Knee: An Indian History of the American West.* New York: Holt, 1970.

Bruer, John. *Schools for Thought.* Cambridge, MA: MIT Press, 1993.

Bruner, Jerome S. *The Culture of Education.* Cambridge: Harvard University Press, 1996.

Bruner, Jerome S. *The Process of Education.* Cambridge Mass.: Harvard University Press, 1963.

Charles, C. M. *Building Classroom Discipline.* Boston: Allyn and Bacon, 2002.

Charles, C. M. *Essential Elements of Effective Discipline.* Boston: Allyn and Bacon, 2002.

Chester, M. D. and B. J. Beaudin. "Efficacy Beliefs of Newly Hired Teachers in Urban Schools." *American Research Journal* 33, 1 (1996): 233-257.

Clayton, J. B. *One Classroom, Many Worlds: Teaching and Learning in the Cross-Cultural Classroom.* Portsmouth, NH: Heinemann, 2003.

Coleman, Daniel. *Emotional Intelligence.* New York: Bantam Books, 1995.

Coleman, Michael C. *Presbyterian Missionary Attitudes toward American Indians, 1837-1893.* Jackson: University of Mississippi, 1985

Coloroso, Barbara. *Kids are Worth It.* New York: Harper Collins. 2002.

Cremin, Lawrence. *American Educator: The Colonial Experience 1607-1783.* New York: Harper and Row, 1970.

Cremin, Lawrence. *The American Common School: An Historic Conception.* New York: Teachers College Press, 1951.

Crow, Tracy M. "The Necessity of Diversity." *Journal of Staff Development* 29, no.1 (Winter, 2008): 54-58.

Cruickshank, Donald, Deborah Jenkins, and Kim Metcalf. *The Act of Teaching.* 4th ed. Boston: McGraw-Hill, 2007.

Cummins, James. "Negotiating Identities: Education for Empowerment in a Diverse Society." *California Association for Bilingual Education,* Ontario, CA, 1996.

D'Angelo, Raymond. *Taking Sides—Clashing Views in Race and Ethnicity, 6th ed.* Dubuque, Iowa: McGraw-Hill, 2008.

Darling-Hammond Land J. Bransford. *Preparing Teachers for a Changing World: What Teachers Should Learn and Be Able to Do.* San Francisco: Jossey Bass, 2005.

Delpit, Lisa. *Other Peoples Children: Cultural Conflict in the Classroom.* New York: The New Press, 1995.

Dewey, John. *Experience and Education.* New york: MacMillan/Collier, 1938.

Doyle, W. "Classroom Organization and Management." In M. Wittrock, ed. *Handbook of Research on Teaching, 3rd ed.* 392-431. New York: Macmillan, 1986.

Doyle, W. *Classroom Management Techniques in O. C. Moles (Ed.), Student Discipline Strategies: Research and Practice.* Albany State University of New York Press, 1990.

Du Bois, W.E.B. *The Souls of Black Folk.* New York: Penguin Books, USA, Inc., 1961.

Duffy, T. and D. Cunningham. "Constructivism: Implications for the Design and Delivery of Instruction." D. Jonassen, ed. *Handbook of Research for Educational Communications and Technology.* New York: Macmillan, 1996.

Duit, R. "Students Conceptual Frameworks: Consequences for Learning in Science." In S. M. Glynn, R. H. Yeany, &B. K. Britton (Eds.), *The Psychology of Learning Science.* Hillsdale, NJ: Erlbaum, 1991.

Eby, Judy. *Reflective Planning, Teaching, and Evaluation for the Elementary School.* New York: Prentice Hall, 2001.

Edmonds, Ronald R. A Discussion of the Literature and Issues Related to Effective Schooling. Cambridge, MA: Center for Urban Studies, Harvard Graduate School of Education, 1979a.

Edmonds, Ronald R. *Making Public Schools Effective.* Social Policy 12 (2), 1981.

Eisenhower, J. S. D. *So Far from God: The U.S. War with Mexico 1846-1848.* New York: Anchor Books, 1989.

Eisner, Eliot. W. *The Educational Imagination: On the Design and Evaluation of School Programs (3rd ed.).* New York: Macmillan, 1994.

Emmer, Edmond T. and Carolyn Evertson. Teacher's Manual for the Junior High Classroom Management Improvement Study. Austin: R&D Center for Teacher Education, University of Texas, 1981.

Emmer, Edmond T. and Carolyn Evertson. *Classroom Management for Middle and High School Teachers, 8th ed..* New Jersey: Pearson, 2009.

Fisher, C., D. Berliner, N. Filby, R. Marliave, L. Cahen, and M. Dishaw. "Teaching Behaviors, Academic Learning Time, and Student Achievement: An Overview." In C. Denham and Lieberman (Eds.), *Time to Learn.* Washington D.C.: Dept of Education, 1980.

Epstein, Joyce L. & M. G. Sanders. "Family, School, and Community Partnerships." In M. Bornstein (Ed.), *Handbook of Parenting (2nd ed.).* Mahwah, NJ: Lawrence Erlbaum, 2002.

Francis, Paul P. *The Great Father: The United States Government and the American Indians.* Lincoln: University Press, 1984.

Freire, Paolo. *Pedagogy of the Oppressed.* New York: Continuum, 1970.

Freire, Paolo. *Education for Critical Consciousness.* New York: Continuum, 1973.

Freire Paolo. *Literacy, Reading the Word and World.* South Hadley, MN: Bergin and Grady, 1987.

Garcia, E. *Student Cultural Diversity: Understanding and Meeting the Challenge, 2nd ed.* Boston: Houghton Mifflin, 1999.

Gardner, Howard. *Frames of Mind: The Theory of Multiple Intelligences.* New York: Basic Books, 1993.

Gay, Geneva, ed., *Becoming Multicultural Educators.* Hoboken, New Jersey: John Wiley and Sons, 2003.

Genovese, Eugene D. *Roll Jordan Roll: The World the Slaves Made.* New York: Vintage Books, 1972.

Geertz, C. *The Interpretation of Cultures.* New York: Basic Books, 1973.

Giroux, Henry. A. *Teachers as Intellectuals: Toward a Critical Pedagogy of Learning.* Granby, Mass.: Bergin and Garvey Publishers, Inc., 1988.

Giroux, Henry. A. *Resisting Difference: Cultural Studies and the Discourse of Critical Pedagogy.* Philadelphia: Routledge, 1992.

Glasser, William. *The Quality School.* New York: Harper and Row Publishers, 1990.

Gollnick, Donna M. and Phillip C. Chinn. *Multicultural Education in a Pluralistic Society.* Pearson: New Jersey, 2006.

Gonzalez, Gilbert. *Chicano Education in the Era of Segregation.* Philadelphia: Balch Institute Press, 1990.

Good, Thomas and T. Beckerman. "Time on Task: A Naturalistic Study in Sixth Grade Classrooms," *The Elementary School Journal.* (1978) 78, 193-201.

Good, Thomas L. and Jere E. Brophy. *Looking in Classrooms, 8th ed.* New York: Addison Wesley Longman, Inc., 2000.

Goodlad, John. *A Place Called School, 20th Anniversary ed.* New York: McGraw-Hill, 2004.

Grant, Carl, ed. *Research and Multicultural Education: From the Margins to the Mainstream.* London: The Palmer Press, 1992.

Grant, Carl, and Maureen Gillette. *Learning to Teach Everyone's Children.* California: Thomson Wadsworth, 2006.

Guadalupe, San Miguel, Jr. *Let All of Them Take Heed: Mexican Americans and the Campaign for Educational Equality in Texas, 1910-1981.* Austin: University of Texas Press, 1987.

Gunstone, R. F., and R. T. White. "Understanding of Gravity," *Science Education.* 1981, 65, 291-299.

Hall, Edward T. *The Silent Language.* Greenwich, Ct.: Fawcett, 1959.

Harris, Ian, M. "Peace Education in a Violent Culture." *Harvard Educational Review* 77, no.3 (Fall, 2007): 350-354.

Hartzopovlos, Maria. "Deepening Democracy: How One School's Fairness Committee Offers an Alternative to Discipline," *Rethinking Schools*, 21, no.1 (Fall, 2006): 42-43.

Helms, J. "Why Is There No Study of Cultural Equivalence in Standardized Cognitive Ability Testing?" *American Psychologist.* 47, 9, (1992): 1083-1101.

Hirsch, E..D. Jr. *Cultural Literacy.* New York: Vintage Books, 1987.

Hofstede, Geert. *Culture's Consequence: International Differences in Work-Related Values.* Beverly Hills, CA: Sage, 1984.

Hunter, Madeline. *Mastery Teaching.* Thousand Oaks, CA: Corwin Press, 1982.

Jackson Lears, Thomas J. *No Place of Grace: Anti Modernism and the Transformation of American Culture 1880-1920.* University of Missouri Press, Columbia Missouri, 1981.

Jacobs, H.H. *Mapping the Big Picture: Integrating Curriculum and Assessment K-12.* Alexandria Virginia: Association for Supervision and Curriculum Development, 1997.

Hom, A, & V. Battistich. "Students' Sense of School Community as a Factor in Reducing Drug Use and Delinquency." Paper Presented at the Annual Meeting of the American Educational Research Association, San Francisco, 1995.

Joshi, Arti, Jody Eberly, & Jean Konzal. "Dialogue Across Cultures: Teachers' Perceptions About Communication with Diverse Families." *Multicultural Education.* 13, no. 2 (December, 2005):11-15.

Johnson, David W. and Roger T. Johnson. *Circles of Learning: Cooperation in the Classroom, 5th ed.* Arlington, Virginia: Association for Supervision and Curriculum Development, 1984.

Kaestle, Carl F. *Pillars of the Republic: Common Schools and American Society 1780-1860.* New York: Hill and Wang, 1983.

Kim, D, D. Solomon, & W. Roberts. "Classroom Practices That Enhance Students Sense of Community." Paper Presented at the Annual Meeting of the American Educational Research Association, San Francisco, 1995.

Kimball, S. T. *Culture and the Educative Process.* New York: Teachers College Press, 1974.

Klopf, Donald W. *Intercultural Encounters: The Fundamentals of Intercultural Communication.* Englewood, Co.: Morton Publishing Co., 1991.

Kohlberg, Lawrence. "Essays on Moral Development." *The Psychology of Moral Development.* 2. New York: Harper and Row, 1984.

Kohlberg, Lawrence. *The Psychology of Moral Development: The Nature and Validity of Moral Stages.* San Francisco: Harper and Rowe, 1984.

Kohn, Alfie. *Punished by Rewards.* New York: Houghton Mifflin Co., 1993.

Kounin, Jacob. *Group Management in Classrooms.* New York: Holt, Rinehart, Winston, Inc., 1970.

Kozol, Jonathan. *The Night is Dark and I am Far from Home.* New York: Simon and Schuster, 1975.

Kuhn, D., E. Amsel, & M. O'Loughlin. *The Development of Scientific Thinking Skills.* San Diego, Academic Press, 1988.

Ladson-Billings, Gloria. *The Dream Keepers: Successful Teachers of African American Children.* San Francisco: Jossey Bass, 1994.

Ladson-Billings, Gloria. "Preparing Teachers for Diverse Populations: A Critical Race Theory Perspective." In A, Iran-Nejd & P.D. Pearson (Eds.), *Review of Research in Education,* 24. Washington, D.C. American Educational Research Association, 1999.

Lansford, Jennifer. "Educating American Students for Life in a Global Society." *Center for Child and Family Policy* 2, no.4 (2002): 1-3.

Lee, James L., Charles J. Pulvino, and Philip A. Perrone. *Restoring Harmony, A Guide to Managing Schools.* Upper Saddle River, New Jersey: Prentice Hall, 1998.

Lee, Robert G. Orientals: *Asian Americans in Popular Culture.* Philadelphia: Temple University Press, 1999.

Lee, Seungyoun, and Mary Ellen Dallman. "Engaging in a Reflective Examination about Diversity: Interviews with Three Pre-service Teachers." *Multicultural Education.* 15, no. 4 (July 1, 2008): 36-44.

Lemann, Nicholas. *The Promised Land: The Great Black Migration and How It Changed America.* New York: Vintage Books, 1991.

Levine, Lawrence W. *Black Culture and Black Consciousness: African American Folk Thought from Slavery to Freedom.* New York: Oxford University Press, 1977.

Likona, Thomas. *Educating for Character.* New York: Bantam Books, 1991.

Likona, Thomas. *Raising Good Children: From Birth Through the Teen Age Years.* New York: Bantam Books, 1983.

Manning, M. L. and L. G. Baruth. *Multicultural Education of Children and Adolescents.* Boston: Allyn and Bacon, 2004.

Marx, Sherry, and Julie Pennington. "Pedagogies of Critical Race Theory: Experimentations with White Preservice Teachers." *Qualitative Studies in Education.* 16, no. 1 (2003): 91-110.

Marzano, Robert J., Debra J. Pickering, and J. McTighe. *Assessing Student Outcomes: Performance Assessment Using the Dimensions of Learning Model.* McREL Institute. Aurora, CO, 1993.

Marzano, Robert J. *What Works in Schools: Translating Research into Action.* Alexandria, VA: Association for Supervision and Curriculum Development, 2002-2003.

McEwan, Barbara. *The Art of Classroom Management: Effective Practices for Building Learning Communities.* Upper Saddle River, NJ: Prentice Hall, 2000.

McGreal, Thomas. *Successful Teacher Evaluation.* Alexandria, VA: Association for Supervision and Curriculum Development. 1983.

McLaren, Peter. *Life in Schools: An Introduction in the Foundations of Education, 5th ed.* Los Angeles: Pearson, 2007.

McLaughlin, W. G. *Cherokee Renascence in the New Republic.* Princeton: University of Princeton Press, 1986.

Ming, Kavin and Charles Dukes. "Fostering Cultural Competence Through School-Based Routines." *Multicultural Education* 14, no.1 (Fall, 2006): 42-49.

Mitchell, Diana. *Children's Literature, An Invitation to the World.* Boston, MA: Allyn and Bacon, 2003.

Monroe, Carla. "Understanding the Discipline Gap through a Cultural Lens: Implications for the Education of African American Students." *Intercultural Education* 16, no. 4 (October, 2005): 317-330.

Moore, John H. *The Emergence of the Cotton Kingdom in the Old Southwest: Mississippi 1770-1860.* Baton Rouge: Louisiana State University Press, 1988.

Nieto, Sonia. *Affirming Diversity: The Sociopolitical Context of Multicultural Education.* New York: Addison Wesley Longman, 2000.

Noddings, Nell. *The Challenge to Care in Schools: An Alternative Approach to Education.* New York: Teachers College Press, 1992.

Noddings, Nell. "Competence and Caring As Central to Teacher Education." Paper presented at the Annual meeting of the American Research Association. Montreal, 1999.

Noddings, Nell, ed. *Educating Citizens for Global Awareness.* New York: Teachers College Press, 2005.

Noddings, Nell. "Teaching the Themes of Care." *Phi Delta Kappan,* 76, (1995): 675-679.

Nuhlicek, Allan. "Relationship of School Boundary Conditions, Gemeinschaft Conditions, and Student Achievement Scores in Reading and Mathematics in Selected Milwaukee Public Schools." Ph.D. diss., Marquette University. Milwaukee, Wisconsin, 1981.

Oakes, Jeannie. *Keeping Track: How Schools Structure Inequality.* New Haven, CT: Yale University Press, 1999.

Oakes, Jeannie and Martin Lipton. *Teaching to Change the World (2nd ed.).* Boston: McGraw-Hill, 2003.

Obeakor, Festus E.. *It Even Happens in Good Schools: Responding to Cultural Diversity In Today's Classrooms.* CA: Corwin Press, 2001.

Ogbu, John. "Cultural Discontinuities and Schooling," *Anthropology and Education Quarterly*, 13, no.4, (1982): 290-307.

Ogbu, John. *Minority Status and Schooling: A Comparative Study of Immigrant and Involuntary Minorities.* New York: Garland, 1991.

Ogbu, John. "Understanding Cultural Diversity and Learning." *Educational Researcher* 21, no.8 (1992): 5-14.

Pai, Y., S. Adler, and L. K. Shadiow. *Cultural Foundations of Education.* Upper Saddle River: Pearson Education, Inc., 2006.

Pai, Y. S., and D. Pemberton. *Findings on Korean American Early Adolescents and Adolescents.* University of Missouri: Kansas City MO, 1987.

Palincsar, A. and A. Brown. "Reciprocal Teaching of Comprehension Monitoring Activities." *Cognition and Instruction* 2 (1984): 117-175.

Perkins, David and T. Blythe. "Putting Understanding Up Front." *Educational Leadership* 51, no. 4 (1992): 4-7.

Perrone,V. ed. *Expanding Student Assessment.* Alexandria, VA: Association for Supervision and Curriculum Development, 1991.

Pewewardy, C. "Learning Styles of American Indian/Alaska Native Students: A Review of Literature and Implications for Practice." *Journal of American Indian Education*, 41 (3), 22-56.

Piaget, Jean. *The Child's Conception of the World.* New York: Harcourt Brace, 1929.

Piaget, Jean. *Origins of Intelligence in Children.* New York: International Universities Press, 1952.

Pickett, Linda. "Diversity Education: Respect, Equality, and Social Justice." *Childhood Education* 84, no. 3 (Spring, 2008): 158.

Power, F.Clark, Ann Higgins, and Lawrence Kohlberg. *Lawrence Kohlberg's Approach to Moral Education.* New York: Columbia University Press, 1989.

Ravitch, Diane. *The Troubled Crusade: American Education, 1945-1980.* New York: Basic Books, 1983.

Ray, Katie. W. "Reading Aloud: Filling the Room with the Sound of Wondrous Words," *Wondrous Words: Writers and Writing in the Elementary Classroom.* NCTE, 1999.

Redfield, Robert. "The Contribution of Anthropology to the Education of Teachers." In F. A. J. Ianni & E. Storey (Eds.) *Cultural Relevance and Educational Issues,* (153-159). Boston: Little, Brown, 1973.

Resnick, Lauren. *Education and Learning to Think.* Washington D.C.: National Academy Press, 1987.

Resnick, Lauren. and I. Klopfer. "Toward the Thinking Curriculum: An Overview." In Resnick and Kloepfer, eds. *Toward the Thinking Curriculum: Current Cognitive Research.* (1989): 1-18.

Reyhner, J., and J. Eder. *American Indian Education: A History.* Norman OK: University of Oklahoma Press, 2004.

Rosenshine, Barak. "How Time Is Spent in Elementary Schools." In C. Denham and A. Lieberman, eds. *Time to Learn.* Washington, D.C.: Department of Education, 1980.

Rosenshine, Barak. "Teaching Functions in Instructional Programs." *The Elementary School Journal,* 83, (1983): 335-351.

Rowe, Mary B. "Wait Time, Slowing Down May be A Way of Speeding Up." *American Educator* 11, (Spring, 1987): 38-43, 47.

Shor, Ira. *Empowering Education: Critical Teaching for Social Change.* Chicago: University of Chicago Press, 1992.

Shor, Ira., and Paolo Freire. *A Pedagogy for Liberation: Dialogues on Transforming Education.* South Hadley, MA: Bergin & Garvey, 1987.

Short, Kathy G., Kathryn Pierce, and Mitchell Pierce, eds. *Talking About Books: Creating Literate Communities,* Portsmouth, New Hampshire: Heinemann Educational Books, 1990.

Sizer, Theodore. *Horace's Compromise: The Dilemma of the American High School.* Boston: Houghton-Mifflin, 1984.

Skinner, B. F. *Science and Human Behavior.* New York: Macmillan, 1953.

Sleeter, Christine, ed. *Empowerment through Multicultural Education.* New York: State University of New York Press, 1991.

Smith, Rogers. *Civic Ideals: Conflicting Visions of Citizenship in U. S. History.* New Haven: Yale University Press, 1997.

Sokolower, Jody. "Bringing Globalization Home, A High School Teacher Helps Immigrant Students Draw on Their Own Expertise." *Rethinking Schools,* 21, no.1 (Fall, 2006): 46-48.

Spindler, G. and I Spindler. *The American Cultural Dialogue and Its Transmission.* New York: Palmer Press, 1990.

Spindler, G. D., "Education in a Transforming America." In G. D. Spindler (Ed.), *Education and Culture* (132-147). New York: Holt, Reinhart, and Winston, 1963.

Spring, Joel. *The American School 1642-2004.* New York: McGraw-Hill, 2005.

Spring, Joel. *Conflict of Interests: The Politics of American Education.* New York: McGraw-Hill, 2005.

Spring, Joel. *Deculturalization and the Struggle for Equality: Dominated Cultures in the United States, 5th ed.* New York: McGraw Hill, 2006.

Stein, S. J. The Culture of Education Policy. New York: Teachers College Policy, 2005.

Stokes, Sandra. "A Partnership for Creating a Multicultural Teaching Force: A Model for the Present." *Multicultural Education* 7, no.1 (Fall, 1999): 8-12.

Strong, R. W., Silver. H.F., and Perini, M.J. *Teaching What Matters Most: Standards and Strategies for Raising Student Achievement.* Alexandria, VA: Association for Supervision and Curriculum Development, 2001.

Takaki, Ronald. *A Different Mirror: A History of Multicultural America.* Boston: Little Brown and Company, 1993.

Taylor, George R., ed. *Practical Applications of Classroom Management Theories into Strategies.* Dallas: University Press of America, 2004.

Thompson, Gail L. *The Power of One: How You Can Help or Harm African American Students.* CA: Corwin Press, 2010.

Tyler, Ralph. *Basic Principles of Curriculum and Instruction.* Chicago: University of Chicago Press, 1949.

Vang, Christopher T. "Minority Parents Should Know More about School Culture and Its Impact on Their Children's Education." *Multicultural Education.* 14, no. 3 (April 1, 2007): 32-40.

Vygotsky, Lev S. *Mind in Society: The Development of Higher Psychological Processes.* Cambridge, MA: Harvard University Press, 1978.

Wang, M.C., G.D. Haertel & H.J. Wahlberg "What Helps Students Learn?" *Educational Leadership*, (1993/1994) 51(4), 74-79.

Whitehead, Alfred N. *The Aims of Education and Other Essays.* New York: Free Press, 1929.

Wiggins, Grant. "Practicing What We Preach in Designing Authentic Assessment." *Educational Leadership*, 54, 4 (1996-1997): 18-25.

Wiggins, Grant & Jay McTighe. *Understanding by Design.* Arlington, VA: Association for Supervision and Curriculum Development, 1998.

Wink, Joan. *Critical Pedagogy: Notes from the Real World.* Boston: Pearson, 2005.

Wong, Harry K. and Rosemary T. Wong. *The First Days of School.* California: Harry T. Wong Publications, 1998.

Zinn, Howard. *A Peoples History of the United States 1492-Present.* New York: Harper Collins, 1999.

Advanced Praise for MASS Professional Development Series

Many of the concepts and principles expressed throughout this Professional Development series were initiated at Bruce-Guadalupe Community School where Dr. Newsome provided consultant services over a five year period to our culturally diverse Latino-American school. The practices were well received by the faculty, community, and students as we opened a new culturally-enriched schooling opportunity for students in the Milwaukee, Wisconsin community. We continue to be grateful to Dr. Newsome for her dedicated work. Readers should find the program which she has outlined in this series to be thoughtful, insightful and practical.

—Walter Sava, Ph.D. Executive Director, Bruce-Guadalupe Community School. Milwaukee, WA

The culturally-centered approach to classroom practice which Dr. Newsome has undertaken in this series is a progressive step forward in pre service and graduate study for our schools of education. It is time to move past the dominant-culture mindset. I agree that we all too often take on the status quo rather than challenging our assumptions and broadening our perspectives about cultures beyond our own. This series is definitely needed in education and beyond.

—Elaine Roberts, Ph.D., Professor, University of West Georgia. Carrollton, GA

Dr. Newsome's unique perspective and approach to classroom practice has been a source of enrichment for me. As a faculty member who worked closely with Dr. Newsome in developing and implementing a key component of this professional development series, I have broadened and systematically incorporated the culturally-transformative approach to teaching in my work with students and into my own teaching repertoire. Readers are sure to change their practices as a result of reading and engaging with the ideas in this series.

—Cathleen Doheny, Ph.D., Professor, Edison State College, Edison, FL

Dr. Newsome's ideas are enlightening to educators everywhere. What I like most about the book series is that it not only covers standard classroom practice, she takes it a step further to discuss how to prepare teachers to operate in a culturally diverse world. She breaks the information down bit by bit in a way that it is extremely understandable to her readers. Her book series is one of my most valuable purchases. I recommend reading it and keeping it as a refresher.

—Mallori Saylor, Student, University of West Georgia, Carrollton, GA

www.ingramcontent.com/pod-product-compliance
Lightning Source LLC
Chambersburg PA
CBHW080552170426
43195CB00016B/2769